PRAISE FOR ~~BEING THE REAL ME~~

Brigitte is a candid storyteller who takes us on a journey of her personal ups and downs and tells us how she found balance in unexpected places... She has the courage to put on paper what most people are afraid to even say out loud-- she might just inspire you!

Christine Soulière, Human Resources Specialist

Inspiring, full of great resources and gives hope for anyone impacted by depression. People will relate to her emotional journey. Highly recommended.

Kevin Lapointe, Co-worker

"Being the Real Me" is exactly who you meet while reading Brigitte Bertrand's autobiography; a woman courageously sharing her story about her struggles through depression and journey back to her true self.

Kim Barnwell CPCC PCC Life Coach
www.conscious-creation.com

It is with great pride that I recommend reading this book. Brigitte did an incredible journey both emotionally and spiritually and she is a great example of courage and determination. Readers who will recognize themselves in her story will also find hope and courage to go through difficult times. I feel privileged to have had the chance to witness part of her exceptional journey.

Gabriel Bergeron, Reiki Master

Being the Real Me

Struggles with Depression

Brigitte Bertrand

BALBOA.
PRESS
A DIVISION OF HAY HOUSE

Balboa Press books may be ordered through booksellers or by contacting:

Balboa Press
A Division of Hay House
1663 Liberty Drive
Bloomington, IN 47403
www.balboapress.com
1-(877) 407-4847

Because of the dynamic nature of the Internet, any web addresses or links contained in this book may have changed since publication and may no longer be valid. The views expressed in this work are solely those of the author and do not necessarily reflect the views of the publisher, and the publisher hereby disclaims any responsibility for them.

The author of this book does not dispense medical advice or prescribe the use of any technique as a form of treatment for physical, emotional, or medical problems without the advice of a physician, either directly or indirectly. The intent of the author is only to offer information of a general nature to help you in your quest for emotional and spiritual well-being. In the event you use any of the information in this book for yourself, which is your constitutional right, the author and the publisher assume no responsibility for your actions.

Some names in this book may have been changed to protect identities.

Printed in the United States of America

ISBN: 978-1-4525-6712-9 (sc)
ISBN: 978-1-4525-6713-6 (e)

Library of Congress Control Number: 2013900993

Balboa Press rev. date: 04/26/2013

Table of Contents

Acknowledgments

I WOULD LIKE TO THANK EVERYONE who participated in one form or another in the creation of this book. I have been blessed to have so much support during this journey. I personally thank each and every one of you, your presence and support meant a great deal to me.

I would like to thank my family and friends for being with me during the difficult times as well as the good times. We have shared many beautiful moments and those memories are the ones I treasure the most. I love you all very much!

To my husband and children, you have always been there for me, but particularly this past year while I worked on this book. You understood the importance of this journey even though it took away from our time as a family. You love me just the way I am, being the real me. I thank you for your encouragement and love. I am grateful to have you in my life and I love you all very much!

For those who accepted the challenge of reviewing my book. I thank you for your expertise, time, and support but more specifically for your honesty. Your valuable feedback has helped me grow as a person but more importantly as an author. I simply could not have done it without you! I thank you all from the bottom of my heart!

To Silvie, I want to thank you for the endless hours you have worked on my book. Thank you so much for believing in me and for believing in this book. Your support was invaluable! I simply cannot find the words to tell you how much this means to me, I am speechless! Je te remercie du fond du coeur!

To Anna, I want to thank you for your editing expertise, your time and recommendations. No words can describe my appreciation. I am blessed to have such a wonderful niece! I love you!

To Myriam, the photographs you took of me where amazing! Thank you so much for making me feel and look so beautiful!

To all my new friends, my support group, thank you for being there! I love you all!

Introduction

I F YOU HAD TOLD ME fifteen years ago that I would write a book, I would not have believed you. If you had told me the book would be my autobiography, I would have laughed at you. It is funny how we really do not know where life will lead us. This book is about faith, destiny, life's challenges, and my depression. It is also about my spiritual journey full of love, truth, and awareness.

I wrote this book with the hope that it would help someone. If I can help one person by sharing my life story, it will have been worth it. If you are going through depression or know someone who is, you might find my book helpful. I share my life story—the good and the bad times—but mainly, I share my experience with depression. I am here to give you hope, to tell you that there is a light at the end of the tunnel. Everyone can suffer through depression, and everyone can come out of depression and live a beautiful life. That is difficult to believe when you are depressed; however, it is the truth. I have always said, "If my journey through depression can someday help someone else, my journey was worth it!" I would not wish depression on my worst enemy, and if this book does help someone, I will be happy, my mission will be accomplished.

Different self-help authors inspired me to write this book: Doreen Virtue and her teachings with the angels, Sonia

Choquette with her guidance on how to trust your vibes, and Louise Hay with her positive affirmations. They inspired me to follow my inner guide; they inspired me by teaching me how to be true to myself. They have showed me the power of following my soul's purpose. They have showed me that, once I truly follow my life's mission, I can be truly happy and whole. These wonderful women do not even know they have inspired me; however, I would like to take this opportunity to thank them. You ladies have changed my life!

This change happened many years after my depression. I wanted to share with you how life has brought me back to my faith and where it has lead me now. I also wanted to share with you how I now live my life with a new sense of spirituality. I followed my inner guidance and my heart when I wrote this book. I simply sat down and wrote whatever came through meditation. I hope that, by sharing my ups and downs, I will inspire you to follow your own inner guidance and learn how to be truly happy. I also hope that you will be able to find happiness by discovering that you are not alone in your journey. I understand what you are going through, and I am there with you. I pray that you (or someone you love) will never have to live through depression, but even if depression strikes, it is worth knowing that others are dealing with similar challenges. I pray for you.

Chapter 1
My Beginning

I AM THE YOUNGEST ONE IN my family. My sister is six years older than I am. We live in the beautiful capital of Canada: Ottawa. My upbringing was Catholic, and my parents were strict. Attending Mass every week was mandatory—even when we were on holiday outside the country. Yes, we went to Mass in Florida, New Jersey, or wherever we vacationed. On Sundays, we had to go to Mass regardless of where we were in the world!

In the 60s and 70s, religion played a great role in many families, especially French Catholic families. Beyond attending church every Sunday, we sometimes went during the week. Needless to say, I went to a Catholic school and participated in all the sacraments. We prayed at home, and we were taught to say our prayers at night before bedtime. There was even a time (when I was eleven or twelve years old) when we would say a prayer before meals. I remember going to restaurants and praying. At that age, such behavior was embarrassing to me. I am not sure whether it embarrassed my sister. Eventually, however, this ritual only occurred on special occasions, such as Christmas, Easter, and Thanksgiving. To this day, we say a prayer before our meals on those holidays.

God had a big presence in our family, especially with my mother—she would go to Mass even on weekdays.

As a child, I started to pray when I was scared or happy. I remember a summer when we visited my uncle at his cottage. He took us on a boat ride, and we found ourselves stranded during a wicked storm. My father and my uncle arranged a shelter for my aunt, mother, cousin, and me by placing the boat's blanket over us. It shielded us from the rain. However, we were still in the water, and the waves were getting bigger. In addition, the lightning and thunder were truly scaring me. I knew that it was dangerous to be on the water when there was lightning. I was scared, so I started to pray the Our Father prayer in order to feel better. This was the only way I could calm myself.

My mother later told me that, when she saw me praying like that, it had made her more nervous! I guess she had taught me well to trust God to protect us, but she had forgotten that part during the storm!

Chapter 2
My Teenage Years

I DID NOT KNOW MANY TEENAGERS who attended Mass. This knowledge did not seem to bother me, though. I would sometime see a friend, and that would be the highlight of my day. All the while, my faith in God did not diminish. I had only one friend who went to Mass as often as I did. Later on, she became one of my closest friends, and we maintain a close relationship to this day.

I was in grade ten when I heard about a special weekend called *La Relève.* This spiritual weekend was about meeting God, finding yourself, and connecting with others. I decided to participate without knowing who was attending.

That weekend changed my life!

I absolutely loved that weekend. I met other teenagers who shared my faith in God, and we shared our personal experiences. I made many friends during that weekend because we all had something in common: we all believed in God and wanted Him in our life. As a teenager, you cannot share these values and experiences with many people—only a few close friends. That weekend made me realize that there were a lot of teenagers that had had similar experiences, and it felt good to know that I was not the only one with faith. Teenagers do not want to stand out in a crowd or be left aside because of their beliefs; therefore, not many will speak about their faith.

On Saturday night, every participant received a letter from God. This letter told us how proud He was of us ... and how much He loved us. This letter made me very emotional! I cried a lot because it made me realize that God was not just a figure of speech in the clouds. He truly exists, and He is truly by your side. You can speak with Him whenever you feel like it, and He will always listen.

I knew that I was no longer alone. I had found friends that shared my beliefs, but most importantly, I had God by my side every step of the way. I spent the rest of my teen years with a great sense of belief in Him. I would say to Him, "*Que ta volonté soit faite,*" which means, "God, I am leaving it in your hands." I would truly leave it to Him and accept whatever came. I would share my grief, ask for His help during difficult times, and feel His presence.

After the weekend of *La Relève,* teenagers and parents met for different activities, such as corn roasts, weekly meetings, summer picnics, and tobogganing in the winter. The group organized a special event, *The Pape Rally,* which was in honor of the pope's visit in 1984 to Ottawa, Canada.

We had workshops during the day. While attending one, I was asked whether I would be interested in receiving communion from the pope. I did not hesitate to accept the offer! What a great honor to be chosen to receive communion from him.

They wanted to capture teenagers receiving communion to show that teenagers were also believers. I was the lucky one, and I received communion from Pope John Paul II. I felt special, as if God had specifically chosen me. I would repeat sayings such as, "*Chaque chose qui arrive a une raison,*" which means, "Everything happens for a reason." I also thought that something positive would always come out of any situation. I truly believed that.

I knew there was a reason why he had chosen me to receive communion; however, I never knew what the reason was. It did not matter. I felt special, and that was enough for me. I remember (at that age) that I wanted to stand out, to become someone extraordinary or special. I told my parents that I wanted to be the first woman to become a Catholic pope! I did not know anything about a soul purpose, but I knew that I wanted to be special—and I wanted to be recognized.

Looking back at those beliefs, I see that I was a very wise girl for my age. I would later somewhat lose that faith, but during that weekend (and beyond) I felt truly protected—I knew I was never in any real danger. I knew that other teens were using drugs at school, but I never saw anyone using, and I was never asked to try them. It was not something that interested me in the first place, and I was never pressured into it. To be frank, to this day, I do not even know what weed smells like! I was never around it. I believe that, through my parents' prayers and God's protection, I was protected … and that is the reason why no one ever approached me.

Because all my friends had boyfriends and I did not, I asked God for a special person in my life. I was often disappointed that I did not have someone in my life. It was not until the end of grade eleven that I got my first boyfriend. He was my first love, and I was head over heels. We went out together for eleven months, and the breakup was truly a heartbreaker! The breakup was my first painful experience. I could not eat, I lost some weight, and I was very depressed. I started to believe that he left me because I was not beautiful or smart enough. I came to think that I was not worthy of being loved. I truly felt rejected. I was not good enough to have a boyfriend. It took me more than one year to recover from that breakup. Thank God I had a best friend who supported me and helped me through that difficult time. It was a good thing that I did not have boyfriends every year—my tender heart would not be strong enough to sustain that much pain. My heart was shattered to pieces!

Chapter 3
My Life as a Young Adult

After high school, I enrolled at the University of Ottawa in the psychology program. I wanted to become a teacher like my sister. I found love again in my first year of university. I was passionately in love! It did not compare to my first love, it was so much more powerful even though it did not last very long. Still, he was truly special to me. We never had any fights but things between us felt off. I wrote him a letter to express my feelings that we were growing apart and when he read it, he expressed he felt the same way. This is when we decided to go our separate ways. I regretted that decision many times. How many times did I think to myself, *Why did you not call him and try to get back?* How many nights did I cry myself to sleep, wishing he would call me back and tell me that we made a mistake. The only reason I never called him and told him I was still desperately in love with him was my pride, my ego. Yes, even at that age the ego interfered in my life, however only in my forties did I learn the real meaning of ego. For many years, whenever I would see him, my heart would jump. He was truly a special person in my life. The lesson he taught me was that beauty came from within. He once told me that it did not matter whether a person was beautiful physically, what mattered was what the person was like on the inside. How true is that! He is a beautiful person, and I thank God for having the opportunity to have him in my life.

In my third year of university, I was asked to teach religion to grade three students before school (at a public school). I was teaching my classes while attending university. I did this for a year and a half. I liked teaching the children; however, I had one group that was more difficult than the others. After class, I was discouraged and exhausted—even though it only lasted forty-five minutes. I wondered how the full-time teacher was able to teach the class every day without going crazy! That was when I realized that becoming an elementary school teacher might not be my calling as I thought.

I was busy during this time. I had three jobs: I was teaching, working fifteen hours per week for a large organization, and working as a receptionist at a legal aid clinic ... all while being a full-time university student. I did not realize it at the time, but I was starting to burn myself out. Like any young adult, I would go out on weekends and dance the night away. I would come back very early in the morning. I needed to sleep in during weekends. I remember having an argument with my father because I wanted to sleep in on Sundays (he expected me to get up and attend Mass with my family). As I said, I had a strict family. I was starting my twenties, and I was still expected to attend church every week. No one else I knew had to go to church every Sunday.

I did not know it then, but that lifestyle had a big impact on my physical being. I became very fragile, especially if I didn't get enough sleep. These experiences ultimately had an impact later on in my life.

As a young adult, my faith continued. I attended spiritual

weekends with others the same age. We met occasionally and discussed our spiritual path, our experience, and ourselves. I continued to go to Mass, and I would pray every night when I went to bed. During one period of time, life was very difficult because I was single. This affected me because I kept asking myself, *What is wrong with me? Am I not pretty enough or good enough to attract a nice man?* My friends were starting to get married, and I had a difficult time getting a date. Some of my friends said that I was too fussy. I did not think so—I was not willing to settle for someone I did not love in order to have a boyfriend. I would mentally make a list of attributes for this special person in my life. I knew what I wanted and did not want.

My mother would tell me, "He is not ready for you; you have to wait for the proper time." She did not want me to get discouraged. She had faith that I would find the right person, and she told me to have faith. Sometimes, I would believe that the timing was not right; however, other times, I would be discouraged and lonely. I remember a particular Christmas when I was sad. I started crying for no apparent reason. It was during dinner, and my whole family was present. I just started to cry, and I did not know why. During my annual exam, I happened to relate this story to my doctor. I said that it must have been the result of Pre-Menstrual Syndrome (PMS). She must have sensed something was off because she referred me to a psychiatrist who was working closely with women affected by PMS. I met with him, and he provided me with medication that would help relieve PMS symptoms. The medication was Zoloft. It seemed to make a difference. I was less sad and less temperamental, especially the week before my period. He made sure to follow up with me, and I would meet with him every month so he could evaluate my condition. I followed that routine for many years.

Today, I question whether it was just PMS, or whether I was suffering from a burnout or depression. I was not paying attention to the signs. I did not know what the signs were. How could I know? I was a young female in my early twenties. Young girls do not suffer from burnouts or depression. How wrong I was! I did not have the knowledge or wisdom I have today, twenty years later. However, my life went on, and I continued to take the medication.

Chapter 4
My Love Story

LOOKING BACK AT THIS PERIOD in my life, I know now that I was not ready to meet him. God tested us by introducing us, but the sparks weren't flying yet! I met Claude when I was working for a large organization (while a student at the university).He was working in Information Technology (IT) support. He came over to fix any computer problems my supervisor had. I was sure that he had a crush on me. How could he not have one? I was cute, funny, and smart. Nevertheless, he never asked me out. For my part, I thought he looked like a nerd—he was not handsome enough for me. One day, I decided to move the process along, so I gave him my phone number on a sticky note. He did not use it for about two years.

After I decided that teaching was not for me, I started to work full time for another large organization.Claude had left the department and would occasionally come to the office to visit his friend, however, and we sometimes bumped into each other. One of those times, he asked me for a lunch date, which I accepted. It happened to be Valentine's Day, and we went to an Italian restaurant. We had a nice time, and the conversation was great—the only problem was the way he looked. He had broken his leg during a hockey game and had a Phentex slipper on his foot along with a cast. This was not the look I wanted for a boyfriend! I still thought he looked too nerdy for me. Why I accepted another date with him, I do not know. A couple of weeks later, we met at the movie theater. His cast was off, but he did not look better … he looked worse! He had a cane! Yes, he walked with a cane like an old man. Now it is funny, but back then, it was embarrassing! I was not ready for my prince charming. God did try more than once to get us together, but for me, the look—the physical body—was more important than the beauty inside. It was truly my loss.

This reminds me of *Shrek*. In the movie, Fiona wants to be rescued by her prince charming, but it is Shrek who rescues her. He is an ogre, and she does not want her prince charming to be an ogre. At the end of the movie, however, she falls in love with him, and the lesson that the children learn is to love with your heart and not with your eyes. The heart doesn't care what the other person looks like. I had to wait another one or two years before he came back into my life.

Destiny plays funny tricks, and we should watch for the signs. The next time I heard from Claude was in the summer of 1991. I had just moved out of my parents' house and into my own apartment. My parents were on holiday, and I was going daily to their house in order to retrieve the mail. One day, as I was bringing in the mail, the phone rang. What you need to know about me is that, every time a phone rings, I must pick it up. I will run in order to answer it in time. Therefore, I had to pick it up—and it was Claude. He was calling to ask me on another date. Talk about destiny! What are the chances that he would call during the two minutes I was inside the house? I decided that I would go with him to the hot air balloon festival and see a concert. We decided on a time, and the following weekend, I met him. Again, I did not understand why I had accepted the date because I was spending the summer with a good friend of mine. We were not really dating, but we *were* spending every minute together. I had had a crush on him since grade seven, and I was hoping to develop a long-lasting relationship with him.

So why did I accept a date with another person if I had my heart set on someone else? I do not have the answer. Today, I can say that my guides were pushing me toward my future husband but I was not ready to accept him. The date was great! We had fun, we laughed, and we realized that we both loved the same song, "Lily Was Here." We saw André-Phillipe Gagnon—a French humorist—and he was great. I think that our relationship could have gone further if I had not had the other person on my mind. The next time that Claude called, I told him that I wanted to pursue a relationship with another person. I told him I was not interested in seeing him at the moment. He did not call back until January of 1994. I do not have to tell you that nothing ever materialized with my male friend (to my utter disappointment), but I am not surprised because he was not the man I was supposed to marry. Shortly after, he started dating his wonderful wife. They are still a wonderful couple today, and our daughters are friends!

I did not date many people after that summer—no one was coming forward, and I was not the type of person to go to a bar in order to meet men. I did not want to meet my husband that way, so I was not wasting my time in bars. As for Claude, little did I know that, whenever he called me, it was because he had broken up with his girlfriend. He decided in December of 1993 to break it off with her for the last time. Of course, a few weeks later, he called. I came back from work one day, and I had a message from him on my answering machine. I thought, *Oh no! The nerd called again!* I did call him back, though. We spoke, and he asked me whether I wanted to go out sometime. I was honest with him, and I said, "Yes, I am willing to go out with you, but only as a friend. We can spend time together as friends, but nothing else. I am really not interested in having a romantic relationship with you." He said that he was okay with that. Therefore, the weekend after, we met at the movie theater. I remember telling my friend that I would not dress up or make myself look nice for him; however, I ended up straightening my hair, which made me look a lot better. When I saw him, my thoughts were, *He does not look like a nerd tonight, and he looks great. What did he do to his hair? He looks nice.*

We had a great evening. We enjoyed the movie, and we spent a lot of time talking. There was no pressure—it was two friends hanging out and having fun. We spent almost every weekend together for the next two months. One weekend in March, I was away to visit a friend. I was surprised at myself because I kept speaking about him, and I realized that I actually missed him. The minute I arrived home on Sunday, I called and asked him to come over. I had missed him more than I was willing to admit. In the following weeks, we had a talk about our relationship and what we wanted it to be. And then he kissed me, and I was blown away! I had butterflies in my stomach. I was falling in love. It is funny how things work.

The only time I was honest with him about being just friends is the time that I actually fell in love with him. I believe it was because we took the time to get to know one another without having any pressure. We realized that we had many things in common, and we actually had fun together! We laughed quite a bit. If you had told me on January 1, 1994, that I would be marrying my prince charming in nine months, I would have told you that you were crazy! However, this is exactly what happened. We fell in love, and we just knew that we were right for each other. I knew exactly what I wanted, and Claude was everything on my wish list. Because I was brought up Catholic, living with a man before marriage was out of the question. We had lengthy discussions about our future, and we both decided that, even though our courtship was not very long, we should get married. We told our families the first week of May that we were getting married in September! Everyone was in shock! I know that, at the office, there were rumors that I was pregnant (they claimed that was the reason why we were getting married so soon). That rumor could not be further from the truth. It took us years to conceive a child!

I remember my mother telling me that when things were meant to be, everything would fall into place. She was right. The wedding arrangements went smoothly. Everything went according to plan. It was God's plan, but I did not know that at the time. I organized a wedding in two months' time, and everything was perfect. Our wedding day was amazing! Nothing went wrong; it was just a wonderful day.

We celebrated in September 2012 our eighteenth wedding anniversary. As I said, when it is meant to be, things work out. When you follow your heart, your soul, and your guides, you are on the right path. It took me sixteen years to learn that valuable lesson, however.

**This is right before the wedding with
my prince charming, Claude!**

Chapter 5

Pongo

Pongo, a few weeks old.

THE FIRST FEW YEARS WERE uneventful. We were getting used to married life, making compromises, having fun. Two years into our marriage, we decided that our condominium was too small, and we wanted to buy a new house. We had one built in Rockland, Ontario. This was an exciting time for us—choosing the layout, the floors, the cabinets, the lights, etc. Our house was built in under three months. We moved in October. This was a great accomplishment: to have our own single family home. We had been there for approximately three weeks when we decided to get ourselves a dog. I saw an ad in the local newspaper for free puppies. I convinced Claude to go and have a look at them. We did not feel obligated to get one, we just wanted to have a look. I don't know whether you've ever gone to see puppies, but they are so adorable! We could not resist ... we had to leave with one! We chose a male. He was black with a small white spot on his nose. His paws looked like they were dipped in white paint! He was so adorable.

I believe that he was just three weeks old, so he was tiny. He could fit between my wrist and my elbow. We brought him home and started to search for a proper name. My nephew suggested we name him Pongo. We loved the name, so we named him that immediately. Pongo became our first-born; he prepared us for parenthood. He was teething ... yes, dogs do lose their baby teeth. In fact, we found one of his tiny teeth on the floor. He chewed on everything: our hands, shoes, and toys! But the best thing we found for him was a wet, frozen facecloth. He would chew on it for long periods, and we could tell that it relieved the pain. We also had to bring him outside in the middle of the night because his bladder was so small. If we did not want any accidents in the house, this was the best thing to do. We also had to carry him down the stairs because he was too tiny to go up or down the stairs by himself. This was funny. We immediately fell in love with him!

He was as precious as any child would be. Pongo was part of the family, and he remained part of the family for a very long time. The best lesson he taught me was that, no matter what, he was always faithful. He never judged us, and he provided us with unlimited love and affection. Just thinking about him makes me choke up. He will be forever in my heart. We found out that, even though Pongo looked exactly like a border collie, he was not. He was a Labrador and collie mix, and his mother did not look like him at all. I believe that he also had the temperament of a border collie. He was the most intelligent dog I ever met. I am not just saying this because he was my dog—I have two golden retrievers now, and they are not as smart as he was.

You might wonder why I go on and on about a dog. There is a very good reason: Pongo played a great role in my recovery from depression. He became one true friend during the dark hours. But before I talk about that period, I want to share with you how smart he was. During the first two years with Pongo, he would always be with us. We brought him everywhere, even to the drive-thru at McDonald's. In fact, the McDonald's in Rockland offered treats to dogs at the drive-thru. No kidding! I had never seen such a thing before, I haven't seen such a thing since. If they saw a dog in the car, they would hand out dog biscuits. It did not take Pongo very long to catch on. Every time we went, his head would be sticking out the window the minute that we lowered it. People loved him. One time, we went to Tim Horton's drive-thru. Pongo did not make the distinction between McDonald's and Tim Horton's. The minute we lowered the window, his head was outside the car. The ladies at the window were surprised, so I explained that, when we went to McDonald's, they gave him dog treats (and thus he was expecting one). She replied, "Wait!" She came back with a doughnut hole and gave it to him!

Chapter 6
My Pregnancy

P ONGO WAS TWO YEARS OLD when I got pregnant. I did not expect to be pregnant because I could not get pregnant for a long time. My husband and I went to specialists and found out we only had a 14 percent chance of conceiving. I was devastated! I wanted children, and finding out that I could not (or even that my chances were very poor) was too much for me to bear. Little did I know that, at the time, the doctor was telling us that we would not likely be able to conceive, I was three weeks pregnant. I found out a month later (when I missed my periods and took a pregnancy test). A miracle had occurred: I was pregnant! We were both so happy!

I started to read books concerning how to familiarize your dog to your babies. This is when we started to set up boundaries in the house. He no longer got any teddy bears to destroy, and he could no longer jump on the bed and sleep with me. This was hard for me, because I loved it when he would jump on the bed and put his tiny head on my tummy. I loved to cuddle with him. The safety of my baby came first, though, so I didn't allow any more jumping on the bed. During the first three months of my pregnancy, I had morning sickness. My husband provided me with a facecloth and sat with me. On the fourth month, the morning sickness went away, but it was replaced by migraines. I would have them, on average, five times per week. The migraines were so intense that I vomited continuously for some days. I even had to go to the emergency room in order to prevent dehydration.

Later on in the pregnancy, the doctors permitted me to use Gravol to stop the vomiting. Such medicine is not recommended in any pregnancy, but my case was too severe—there was nothing else that would stop me from being sick. Even with that medicine, I spent a lot of time in the bathroom being sick, and I got migraines at least five times per week. Claude would always be by my side—except once. On that occasion, Pongo noticed and decided that I should be accompanied. He went to Claude and barked at him. Claude asked him, "What, Pongo?" Pongo then proceeded to the bathroom, watching behind him to make sure that Claude was following. He was telling him, "This is your job; you need to stay with her!" We were so amazed by his actions. We could not believe that a dog would notice his absence and make sure that Claude came to me. His behavior reminded me of Lassie.

The best thing that Pongo ever did, however, occurred on the night that my labor started. I started my contractions around half past eight o'clock at night. I went to bed around ten o'clock, but I could not sleep. I went downstairs to the family room to watch television while Claude was still sleeping. Pongo stayed with me in the family room. He never left my side except when, at two o'clock in the morning, my contractions became stronger and closer to five minutes apart. I told Pongo, "Go upstairs and wake up Daddy." He went upstairs, and then he returned downstairs alone. I replied, "No, Pongo, go upstairs and get Daddy. Bring Daddy downstairs." He went back upstairs and finally came down with my husband. Claude later explained to me that, the first time he went to see him, he woke him up, but he ignored him. However, the second time, Pongo woke him up and would not move until Claude got the message. Again, Claude asked him, "What, Pongo?" Pongo then proceeded to the door while looking behind, making sure that Claude was following him. He brought my husband down for me! We were amazed that he truly understood what I asked him to do—and he delivered. He was an exceptional dog. My two goldens would never be able to do such a thing. He was a smart dog.

Chapter 7

Cassandra

CLAUDE CAME DOWNSTAIRS AND STAYED with me throughout my labor and during the delivery. I started my contractions Saturday night, and I had Cassandra Sunday at 2:35 p.m. She was perfect! My miracle baby was born.

She slept for long periods, and she rarely cried. I believe that, by two months, she was sleeping through the night. All the while, I was breastfeeding Cassandra, and it became overwhelming to be at her beck and call. I was also having difficulty breastfeeding. I had a hard time getting used to the technique and it was very painful. However, I was determined to breastfeed because I knew that was the best thing for my baby but it did take a toll on me. That is when I started to feel the blues. I believe that during the first few months of her baby's life every woman goes through a time when she gets the blues.

I noticed that I was not myself on my birthday. Usually for my birthday my family comes over, I go out to a restaurant; I simply get pampered because it is my special day. However, I did not want to be pampered that year! I did not even want to have my family around. That was unusual for me; I was feeling depressed and overwhelmed. You think nothing of it because you read in the pregnancy books that it is perfectly normal to have the blues after the delivery, so you just go with the flow. Cassandra was always smiling; she was a true pleasure to have.

Cassandra, smiling as always. The perfect baby!

After the delivery, I went back to the doctor for a checkup. He asked me what my plan for contraception was. I simply answered that I had none. Our chance to conceive was only 14 percent, so what was the point in taking precautions? Well miracle number two happened! I got pregnant again when Cassandra was only six months old. This was a huge surprise—one that was not prepared for. However, we were really happy with the news.

If we put things in perspective: I was pregnant and having more migraines with this pregnancy, and I still had a baby to take care of. In addition, my hormones were making me sad all the time. At one point, I told my husband that if I were not pregnant, I would just bury myself in the ground. This is when both my husband and I became aware that I was truly not well, that I needed help.

I was tired and restless as I took care of my baby. Of course, I loved her and cherished every moment with her, but something inside me was not right. I had difficulty coping with what life was sending me. I was blocked by something. Was it love? Fear? Exhaustion? I do not know, but I was tired all the time—even after sleeping twelve hours. I could not get myself back on track. I could not get any energy, and I was drained by something—as if something was sucking energy out of me even before I received it. Looking back, I know that the name of what was happening to me was depression. Why would a thirty-year-old woman who just gave birth to a gorgeous, healthy baby girl (and was happily married) be depressed? I have no idea, and I did not have the answer then either. Depression does not choose sad people; it does not discriminate—it can happen to anyone. Yes, even the ones who have everything to live for.

Chapter 8
I Need Help!

I BELIEVE THAT THE TRIGGER WAS my hormones. Because of the pregnancy, they were all screwed up … and they were screwed up for a very long time. These hormones were controlling my life! I did smile and laugh occasionally, but not fully. Something inside me was missing. I was telling myself that I could not be depressed because I still laughed. That is another myth, that you cry all the time when depressed. In reality, you can be depressed and have short periods during which you laugh or smile. However, those periods are few and far between. I could not understand what was happening to me. I felt like a failure, and I was having a difficult time taking care of my baby, my house, and my job. My body did not have a chance to return to its normal self. My hormones were crazy. You might think that is normal for a pregnant woman. Maybe, but for me, the baby blues that had started after Cassandra's birth became stronger and pulled me into complete darkness. I was experiencing a major depression. I overreacted to everything, such as my child's welfare or my colleagues' feedback. I almost (or maybe I did) became paranoid. It was worse at the office—I felt like everyone was against me.

To be frank, I do not recall how I got the number at the hospital. I believe that my gynecology doctor may have provided me with the number for the mental health section of the Ottawa Hospital. Regardless, I called. A couple of weeks later, I was seeing a psychiatrist at the hospital. On the first visit, they made me fill out a questionnaire. It determined the level of my depression. The questionnaire indicated that I was suffering from a major depression. The problem was the treatment. They could not cure the disease without prescribing medication, but they could not provide me with any medication because I was pregnant (and it would affect the baby's health). The only thing they could do was monitor my situation closely. The doctor saw me twice per week. It was not working very well. In addition, the clinic at the hospital could only see patients for a small amount of time, and they had to refer the patient to an out-clinic. Because of my situation, the psychiatrist made an exception and kept seeing me until I had the baby. Once I delivered, I had to find an out-clinic for counseling. When I had Pierre-Hugues, the psychiatrist came to see me, wished me well, and provided me with telephone numbers for out-clinics. That was the last time I saw her. Today, I think that alternative medicine would have been helpful in my case. It is so unfortunate that doctors rarely recommend alternative medicine such as acupuncture. I am positive that it would have helped with my depression—and it would not have harmed the baby.

Chapter 9
Pierre-Hugues

As for my new baby boy, he came out crying, and he did not stop for almost three months. He had colic, and nothing would relieve him or make him stop crying. Nursing would sometimes help, but I could not nurse him twenty-four hours per day! He was the total opposite of Cassandra.

Imagine a depressed mother with a new baby who cried constantly and a fourteen-month-old daughter who could barely walk by herself. That was my life! I had a hard time sleeping because my son was crying all the time, and he only slept for short periods of time. Thank God, my husband was at home during that time and helped me with my daughter and the meals. Also, during the night, he brought Pierre-Hugues to the bed so I could breastfeed him. However, this only lasted a few weeks because he had to go back to work. Nevertheless, during that time, I could rest in bed while breastfeeding. And when Pierre-Hugues woke up for his second feeding, I would be right there.

**This is a picture of a depressed woman
with her baby. Can you tell?**

I remember one night—as I was standing beside the crib, looking at my son sleeping—I was crying and feeling guilty for not feeling anything. I remember saying to my husband, "I cannot bond with him." With my daughter, it had been instantaneous. My love for her was immense right from the start. However, for him, I just could not feel anything. I felt like a terrible mother because I had not yet bonded with my child. I was feeding him, changing him, and bathing him, but I could not feel a strong connection with him. I believe it was because he was crying all the time. How many times did my husband and I wish he would stop crying? I do not quite remember the exact moment I bonded with him but I guess it is when he stopped his colics, which would be when he was three or four months old. Today, my son and I share a special bond. I love him with all of my heart! I am lucky because I have two wonderful children whom I cherish and love immensely.

At one point, I was exhausted, so I asked my husband to pick him up and try to comfort him. Pierre-Hugues would have none of that. He would start crying louder until I held him in my arms. He only wanted his mother. What a stress on a mother! Now add a depressed mother! Even in my arms, he would cry, but it seemed like the cries were quieter. The whole responsibility was on me to nurse him and comfort him. This became a tough situation for my husband and me. I wanted him to take care of my son, but when he did, Pierre-Hugues screamed so loud that I wanted to take him back. My husband felt frustrated that he could not comfort his son. It was not easy having a very depressed mother and a very discouraged dad in the same house.

Throughout this mess, we were lucky. Yes, we were very lucky to have such a wonderful daughter. She was a happy baby. She was smiling all the time, sleeping through the night—and she loved to baby her little brother. She would try to comfort him as well by giving him kisses! She was such a sweetheart!

**Cassandra is hugging her baby brother,
Pierre-Hugues. How precious!**

Because Pierre-Hugues was such a difficult baby, we decided to continue sending Cassandra to her babysitter. This left me with fewer responsibilities at home. I was alone with Pierre-Hugues and could rest when he would rest. My husband brought her to the babysitter every morning and picked her up at night after work … and then he came home to cook dinner. Because I was physically and emotionally exhausted, my husband had to help me with everything (even though he had to go to work).

I think Pierre-Hugues was three months old when he slept more than three hours during the night. We were happy with that improvement, but every night he would still have colic and cry for three or four hours. I was fed up. I wanted to run away from all the responsibility and sleep for a year! I was tired of having Pierre-Hugues in my arms whenever he would cry. My parents were in Florida at the time. I asked—begged—Claude to join me on a trip there. He did not feel comfortable leaving a three-month-old baby and a seventeen-month-old toddler. He wanted to stay with them, but he agreed that I should take a little vacation. I decided to leave my family for a week. That decision came after I had consulted my psychiatrist. He convinced me to stop breastfeeding my son in order to start taking medication, and he wanted me to sleep as much as possible. I needed to do that in order to beat my depression.

I joined my parents in January. I think I cried every day. I missed my family, and I wished I could be with them. The only time I was not depressed, was when I went shopping. I did shop a lot during that week. I bought many clothes for the children at the fashion outlets. During that time, I felt lighter—almost free. Still, I slept through the night and late into the morning, but the fatigue did not disappear. It was as if I were dragging a sixty-pound backpack all the time. However, I could not complain because I was not hearing a baby crying. I would call them every day and cry. Did the vacation cure my depression? Not at all. Did it help me? Possibly. Did it help Claude's relationship with Pierre-Hugues? Yes! It did wonders! The boys were able to bond, and finally, my husband was able to comfort his son. Pierre-Hugues did not have any choice in the matter because I was not there—he had to take the comfort that his father was giving him. They got to spend a lot of time together, getting to know each other. Upon my return, whenever Pierre-Hugues had his colic, he would accept being held by his father. That was a huge relief for me.

Chapter 10

Full Depression

THE MEDICATION I HAD STARTED to take was still not working. Even after about six weeks, I did not notice any improvements. An important side effect of the medication was weight gain. I felt even more depressed because I was now overweight!

The psychiatrist recommended having both children in daycare in order for me to recuperate. I did not take that news very well. I would be consumed with guilt. How could a mother send her two children to daycare while she stayed home and did nothing? That was inconceivable to me. However, I did follow the doctor's advice, and I changed the medication at least four times before we found the right one for me. It took a year—yes, a year—to find the proper medication for me. This is an eternity for someone suffering from depression. And during that time, I received no relief, the symptoms were still present. Life continued as if I was not taking any medication. During that year, I took care of two babies without being physically or mentally capable. I just wanted to die. I was trying to think of the easiest way to end my life. One day, my husband found me crying in the kitchen with a bottle full of different prescription drugs. I was prepared to take them in order to stop the nightmare.

The only hesitation I had before taking the medication was the thought of my children. I felt sad that they would never know their mother. I asked myself some questions, *Who will take care of them besides Claude? Will he remarry?* I was sure that he would, and I could not fathom any other woman taking care of them. I was jealous that my husband would find someone to replace me. Those thoughts were going through my mind as I was holding the bottle in my hands and crying. No, not crying—bawling. He stopped me in time and threatened to bring me to the hospital if I did not control myself. What went through my husband's mind when he found me? I do not know, I never asked him. If I were to ask him today, I am not sure that he would want to answer. I do not think he wants to think about that period in our lives. He must have felt despair. He must have asked himself, *What do I do with her now?* There are no textbooks that tell you how to take care of someone who is depressed or suicidal. In retrospect, he probably should have called the doctor or the hospital. Maybe that would have provided me with more care.

I did not want to go to a mental hospital; I just wanted to be free of my disease. I wanted energy; I wanted to be happy. I was tired of being exhausted and crying all the time. I took the telephone numbers for the outpatient clinic and found myself a therapist. I wanted help, so I went once per week to meet with the therapist. I was under the care of a psychiatrist, and I was now in psychotherapy. I believe she was there just to listen. Did she provide me with advice? She did. She tried to provide me with a different perspective on my life, on Claude. However, I remember clearly that she felt that I was alone in my battle. She felt that Claude was not supporting me during my illness. That was a shock to me. When I realized that I was truly alone, I started to feel resentful toward others because they had abandoned me during my time of need. It might have helped me to meet with other people who were going through the same thing as me, but she never referred me to group therapy. Did everyone really abandon me? Not really, they just did not know what to do or what to say. Claude was there physically and emotionally, and he tried his best. It was not enough for me, however—even though it was all he could do. And how can you ask someone for more? In retrospect, I believe that anyone going through what he went through should be followed by a therapist. He needed coaching, assistance, and support from someone. The therapist could have helped, and he or she could have given him tools in order to help him deal with me. We did go to couple's therapy, but Claude felt that they were always telling him to shut up and take whatever I was sending his way, because I could not help it. How could he heal and take care of me if he did not have any support for himself?

He was coping the best way he could, and he made mistakes (like me). As I said, he was there physically for me but he could not connect with me emotionally. He could not be compassionate, as he did not understand the illness. I remember telling him that he did not "get it". I tried to explain to him "if you were to see me with a broken leg, you would see that I am in pain and that it is physically challenging for me to move. You would feel compassion towards me. Being depressed is the same thing, my soul is broken and I cannot function physically, but you treat me as if there is nothing wrong with me because you cannot see with your eyes what is wrong with me. You cannot see what is broken." I was broken but no one was seeing it, no one was getting it. This was causing me a lot of pain. The fact that people could not acknowledge that I was ill was painful for me. There was a lot of resentment and conflict in our relationship because he was neither compassionate nor understanding. I was upset and frustrated with him. I thought that he did not love me, as he should. I thought that he did not appreciate me nor the efforts I made daily.

On the other side, Claude also had issues with me. He also felt resentful because I did not appreciate everything he did. I did not comprehend the burden he was carrying by himself. He had to carry all the pressure in the relationship. He was the one that made sure that the bills were paid on time, that the household chores were done, that the children were well taken care of. Before the depression, we were equally responsible for everything. Now all of these responsibilities were his whether he liked it or not. I did not appreciate the efforts he was making. I did not understand how much these responsibilities were a burden on him. I was ungrateful and he resented me. This was very difficult for our relationship as the anger was gradually building up to a point where it was very tense in our household. We were no longer a loving couple. We said things to each other that were not nice. Words can hurt very deeply sometime. I do not recall the words but I remember that we were both hurt. The overall experience affected our marriage enormously.

Those years almost destroyed our relationship. It was not just a bump in the road, it was a major hurricane! It left our relationship dismantled, in thousands of pieces. How did we survive? Was our love enough? We no longer had trust—I could not trust him to always be there for me. He was taking care of himself first, by starting to go out with friends at night in order to find relief and support while I wanted him home with me and the children. His actions did not show me that he loved me no matter what. He had to be selfish though… he had to take care of himself first in order to be able to cope with the children and me. I get that now. I did not then. I was too hurt by his actions to fully understand what he was going through. In my mind, it needed to be about me, what I needed. I was the one sick, not him. That is not reality; that is the illusion that the illness gives you. Still, that was my perspective for several years after my depression and we came very close to separation.

I did not see many friends during that period. Not many people could relate to me or even begin to understand what I was going through. Even my family had a hard time. They truly wanted to help me, but they did not know what to do or what to say. It seemed to me that everything they said was the wrong thing to say to me. That was my perception of things. It does not mean that what they said was wrong, however; it just means that I took it the wrong way. Therefore, I did not seek their support. I did see them and interact with them, but they were not the people I wanted to reach out to.

I had one good friend who was always there for me, and I felt comfortable reaching out to her. She listened without judgment. That was exactly what I needed: a shoulder to cry on. We spoke every week, and occasionally, we met for lunch or went shopping together. Whenever I was upset, she was the person I called. She was my rock!

Once, when I was truly upset with my husband and wanted to punish him (or maybe just get a reaction out of him). I decided to leave the house without telling him. I did this late in the evening. I was driving while crying, and I did not know where to go. I even contemplated crashing the car—that would end all the pain. Once I started to think it over, I realized that the insurance company would not pay any life insurance if it were a suicide. I did not want to put Claude into a financial hardship, so I decided not to pursue that option. I continued to drive and ended up at Julie's place. Her husband opened the door and let me in. I wonder what he was thinking. Who goes to someone's house at eleven o'clock at night crying? Though Julie was compassionate, she also wanted to warn Claude that I was safe at her place. I did not want her to call him because I wanted him to worry about me. She listened to me once again without judgment and tried to reassure me that everything would get better.

Claude did find me; he called not long after I arrived. He told me to call my parents because they were worried about me. He had called them first expecting me to be there. I had to call them to reassure them that I was fine and would go back home. After speaking for a few hours, Julie wanted me to stay overnight. Unfortunately, I knew that was not an option for me because Claude was working the next day and needed the car (we only had one car at that time). Julie made me promise to drive carefully and not try anything stupid. I convinced her that, if I wanted to end my life, I would have done it before going to her place. I called her once I arrived home to tell her that I was fine. I was truly blessed to have such a friend in my life.

I do not recall whether I had a discussion with Claude about why I was so upset with him. I just remember that I wanted to scare him. Did it work? Probably. Would I recommend such behavior? Absolutely not—I do not recommend putting your loved ones through such stress. They suffer as much as you do, you just do not recognize it. They have to be strong for you because you can no longer function normally. The perception of a depressed person is different from a healthy person. Once you are out of the depression, you realize how much your perception was twisted. You may even be paranoid—I was!

My other friend was my dog, Pongo. He loved me unconditionally and was there for me. As I previously mentioned, he was a smart dog, and he could sense when I was upset. He would come to me and use his nose to nudge me to pet him. This was his way of saying that he was there for me. He would also try to lick the tears coming down my face. Pongo was not an affectionate dog by nature. Yes, he did like to be petted, but he did not want me to pet him for too long. If I did pet him too long, he would start to growl. I used to laugh at him whenever he started to growl. I would say, "I know you want me to stop. I can hear you say, 'Mom enough of this!'" However, he never growled when I was upset. Instead, he would continue to stand beside me and let me pet him. It is as if he knew that the motion of petting him was soothing for me. Feeling his heartbeat by my side gave me a sense that I was no longer alone, that he was there with me, and that he loved me. I needed to feel loved and appreciated, and he was able to give that to me. As I said, he gave me unconditional love. He was truly a blessing. I did not realize it, but he made me exercise. He was an active dog and needed his walks, so he would tell me whenever he wanted to go out. We had a wooded area behind our house, and Pongo loved to walk into those woods. We took many walks together. That was good for me because it got me outside of the house and doing exercise. I never enjoyed exercise, but I did love to take long walks in those woods with him.

At that point, it was obvious that I could not go back to work. My children were at daycare because I could not take care of them. I was still physically and emotionally exhausted, even when Pierre-Hugues was six months old and the medication was still not working. Claude finally agreed to hire someone to clean the house. They came every other Friday from eight o'clock to noon. I was upset because, on those Fridays, I could not sleep in—I had to get up at eight o'clock and leave the house. Unbelievably, that was a huge deal for me! It was really demanding. My friends did not understand. How could I complain about getting out of bed early in order to have my house cleaned? Only someone who is suffering from depression can understand the extent of the exhaustion. Even getting dressed in the morning is very demanding for someone who is depressed. You hardly have any energy left in you to fix yourself breakfast. I do not know whether I can compare this situation to one in which someone is terminally ill, but to me it felt like that. Every movement of your body is extremely demanding. Try adding a hundred pounds into a backpack and carrying it for days—that will give you an idea of how it felt to me.

Depression is not just being sad and crying. The exhaustion is the worst. For me, constantly feeling tired (even after sleeping twelve hours and doing nothing during the day) was a nightmare. On the good days, I would get out and see people or go to the mall and spend money—money I did not have. It did not matter whether I had money or not, it just made me feel good—like when you eat junk food. You know that it is not good for you, but it fills a hole and makes you feel temporarily better. Sadly, the darkness always returned … sometimes twice as bad because I felt guilty. So instead, I started to buy things for the children. I figured that if it was for the children, it would be acceptable.

My husband was good about it. He never complained that I spent too much (even though we did not have money to spare).

I am sure that he felt stressed about me spending our money, but he never mentioned anything (probably because he did not want to burden me with more distress). Since I was on sick leave, I was only earning 70% of my salary from the Disability Insurance. You have to realize that depression does not only affect you, it affects people that surround you. My husband had to keep it together—not just for me, but also for our children. He had a family to take care of. Since I could not help him, he had the whole responsibility on his shoulders. Today, I know that it was a heavy weight to place upon him. And that weight forever changed him. It was almost like being a single father, except he did have a wife. Of course, instead of helping him, I needed to be taken care of.

I have said already, that he had to wake up in the middle of the night to bring me Pierre-Hugues for his feeding. He also changed his diaper at that time. And then, once morning came, he had to get the children ready, bring them to the babysitter, and go to work. He worked a full day, and then the routine started again: pick up the kids at the babysitter, get home, cook dinner, help with the baths and feeding, put the kids to bed, and do whatever needed to be done at home. Only then could he go to bed. He would hope that, during the day, I would not break down again. If I did, that meant that he would need to calm me down and be subject to my verbal abuse. He could not try to reason with me—you just cannot do that with people suffering from depression. It is as if the capacity for reason has been taken away from them. They just see the worst in every situation, and it is everyone else's fault. I cannot recall my conversations with him, but he told me later on that I complained that everything he did was wrong. That did take a toll on his self-worth and his mental state. He started to feel depressed himself; it is as if my depression was rubbing off on him. My psychiatrist started to see both of us in order to make sure that Claude would not suffer deeper from depression. He provided him with a medical certificate and recommended that he take four to five weeks off in order to recuperate. Meanwhile, I complained all the time. I asked him to reassure me, to comfort me, to hug me, to tell me I was great. Today, it is hard for me to understand that state of mind—and I lived through it! Once you are out of your depressive state, you forget those details.

Chapter 11
Losing your mind

I HAVE TO SAY THAT, WHEN you are depressed, you have no memory. It is as if someone deleted that function from your brain. When people ask me details about my son's first few years of life, I rarely can answer. I can remember vivid details about Cassandra's first year, though. For example, I remember the first time that Cassandra laughed. She was three months old, and we were in her bedroom. I was reading her a story while rocking her. She suddenly saw Pongo come into her room, and she just started to laugh. It was a laugh that came from the belly. When he disappeared, she stopped laughing. Claude then got Pongo to come back into the room, and the minute he did (and she saw him again), she started again, laughing really hard. It was hilarious! We laughed so much that we had tears in our eyes. That was a precious moment. Our beloved Pongo made our baby laugh for the first time. To this day, Cassandra loves dogs. Sadly, I cannot remember anything similar with my son. Depression stole that from me. I cannot recall the first time he smiled at us or his reaction to Pongo. When was the first time he ate solids, or took his first step, or lost his first tooth? I do not recall any of it.

I also have a difficult time remembering where God was during this difficult time. Did I lose my faith during my depression? Did I pray during these difficult times? Oddly, I cannot recall any of those memories. I cannot even recall if we still attended church. My only recollection of God during this period is of my children's christening. Both my children were baptized when they were infants. This tells me that I must have still believed in God however, I do not know if I was still praying every night. I do not recall feeling Him near me during my depression. Today when I reflect back on this period, I know that God was with me every step of the way. He did not abandon me; I just did not see it then.

I forgot so many things. How many times did I call Claude in a panic because I had forgotten where I had parked the car? Many times! If I did not immediately see the car, I would panic and call Claude. I do not know whether I was having anxiety attacks, but my heart was beating extremely fast, and I could not concentrate. Claude could not tell me where the car was, but he was able to calm me down until I eventually found it. As I describe these episodes, I feel so silly. I could not cope with any pressures, regardless of how small they were. It goes to show you how someone who is suffering from depression does not have a viable coping mechanism. Small events can put enormous pressure on the person.

Decisions were also very difficult to make during this time. For example, while at the grocery store, I could not decide which product to buy. I still see myself with two cans of tomatoes in my hands and tears in my eyes because I could not choose which one to buy. I called Claude (thank God for cell phones!) and asked him which one to buy. I wonder what he was thinking? He needed to be patient with me. I do not recall how long I acted that way—as I told you, I've lost many details of my life. I am just glad that I've moved past those times!

Chapter 12
Relief, Healing, and Forgiveness

O NCE WE FOUND THE PROPER medication, life became
easier. The darkness started to lift gradually. Medication
does not change your life immediately, though. The negative
emotions become less severe, but the fatigue stayed much longer.
And the self-pity stays with you until the healing process is
complete. You must heal from depression. The medication is a
lifesaver—it takes away the dark clouds—but you are still left
with a wound. You need to continue with your therapy in order
to fully heal that wound.

Eventually, you will only see the scar that your depression has
left, but that takes time. It took me many years of psychotherapy
in order to fully heal. What you must understand is that, during
this dark period in your life, you are wounded easily. It is as if
your immune system is not functioning, and you get bruised
easily. Until your immune system is back to normal, you will
accumulate wounds that will need healing. This work needs
to happen with your therapist. I needed many years to build
back the trust with my husband. It was not an easy process,
but I believe we became a stronger couple. Our love was able to
keep us together. We had to look inside ourselves and truly see
what needed fixing. Sometimes, we did not want to go there,
however—we just wanted to bury whatever hurt us and move

on. But that is not how you heal. You must look at the situation and find a way to forgive yourself and your partner. In short, forgiveness is how you heal. This is huge! I was only able to forgive myself a year ago for being sick and not taking care of my children. I had to forgive myself for being weak. I had to accept that I was (and am) a great mother. Back then, I did not understand that not being a good mother would have been staying at home with the children (thus not providing them with the best care). Being a bad mother would mean screaming at the kids because I was tired and could not stand their demands. Instead, someone else was taking care of my babies while I was trying to take care of myself by sleeping and resting. Not to discourage anyone, but in my case, I would say that the tiredness persisted for approximately ten years. I never got better until I drastically changed my life. I will explain later what I did. Yes, forgiveness is part of the healing process, but there is much more to it.

Chapter 13
Return to Work

G RADUALLY, WITH THE HELP OF medication, I found myself again. I started to do more with the children and in the home. Little by little, I took on more responsibility, and eventually, I needed to get back to work. I had been away from work for one and a half years. My psychiatrist recommended that I return slowly. I needed to coordinate my return to work with the disability insurance company. I met with my coordinator, and we established a gradual return to work schedule based on the recommendation of my doctor. I needed to take baby steps, so I started with half a day per week. That sounds like nothing, but for me, it was immense. My energy was still not 100 percent, so just getting up and dressing took a lot of energy. The drive to the office in the morning traffic also ate up my energy, so by the time I actually got to work, I did not have much energy left in me. I do not recall whether it was one or two weeks later, but soon, I began working one full day at the office. I did that for a few weeks before increasing the time to one and a half days.

It took me a full year before I reached four days per week. I worked three days per week at the office and one day at home. That schedule was not well received by my supervisor at the time, but he knew that he needed to accommodate my condition. Still, despite having my psychiatrist's evaluation, he wanted me to be assessed by a medical specialist. I did not know then that I could refuse that evaluation, so I went along with the request. I met with another psychiatrist, and it was not a pleasurable experience. He asked me questions for an hour, and then he sent a report to my employer. The report stated that I was not fit to return to work and the medication my doctor prescribed was not proper. He recommended that I take a different medication. I was furious! He saw me for an hour—he did not know me. My psychiatrist had followed me for years, and I felt that he was better equipped to make an assessment than the new person. My psychiatrist was also not impressed with the report, stating that the recommended medication was not at all effective. Not knowing what to do, I spoke with my insurance representative and asked her how she wanted me to proceed. I wondered, *Should I go back to work against the specialist's recommendation or stay home despite my original doctor's views?* Finally, it was decided that I was fit for work and recommended that I work one day at home. All that time and negative energy to get back to the original schedule! I hope that my manager felt more comfortable with my situation after putting me through that ordeal.

I stayed with that department for only one year. I did not like the work, and I didn't feel that I contributed anything positive. I met with a previous manager whom I had worked for, and she convinced me to return to human resources. She said that, instead of working as a staffing assistant, I should be a staffing advisor. That was an excellent move—I loved it! My depression was under control, I gained more energy every day, I felt less tired, and I loved my new job. After three years, I could say that I was happy. I felt good about myself, and I started to lose some weight. Everything seemed to be getting back to normal. I still work four days per week. I tried to work five days, but every time I did, the depression symptoms returned. For my well-being, I made the decision to never go back to working five days per week. This schedule provides the best work/health balance for me. I also notice that, if I change my routine significantly, I will start to feel the symptoms reappear. My body is more fragile than it was twenty years ago—I need to listen to it.

Chapter 14
Weight Gain

I WANT TO MENTION THAT, WHEN depressed, you seek unhealthy foods. These foods range from salt and vinegar chips to pizza to fries to candy to chocolate—anything that is not good for you. In addition, during the first year (when I was trying different kinds of medication), I gained a lot of weight. Yes, antidepressants do make you gain weight, which does not help your emotional condition. You already feel depressed, and when you gain weight, you are even more depressed because you now feel and look awful! This reality can damage your self-esteem.

Many people I have met who suffer from depression (and gained weight due to medication) have not had the strength to change their diet and lose weight. You need to concentrate on one thing at a time, and the priority is to get better emotionally, not physically. I was overweight for approximately a year and a half. Never before did I weigh so much. My family always struggled with weight, but not me—until depression hit, anyway. I could tell that my father was worried because he struggled with weight gain all his life, and he did not want me to experience the same thing.

Once the medication started to work, I decided to go on

Weight Watchers. Once I made my decision, there was no going back for me. I decided to follow the diet and stick with it. Surprisingly, the plan that Weight Watchers recommended was easy to follow, and I could still eat what my family was eating (while watching my portions). Every week, I lost some pounds and felt proud of myself. Six months later, I realized I had lost forty pounds. I felt great about myself. I looked great—and my medication was working—so my morale was also improving. I had gone back to work, and my life was starting to feel normal again. I have read many times that weight gain is closely related to emotional challenges. Many people are emotional eaters, and I am one of them—that fact has been proven.

I have to admit that weight gain will always be a struggle for me. At the time of this writing, I am overweight by at least fifteen pounds. My colleagues do not believe me when I tell them that, but I know what my healthy weight should be. Because I am short—just five feet tall—I cannot afford to put on some pounds. I have tried many yo-yo diets, but I continue losing weight only to gain it back after six months or a year. I try to eat healthy foods and limit my portions, though. Hopefully, one day, I will be able to maintain a healthy weight. I try not to let my weight affect my self-esteem, though. The beauty of a person is found within him or her. I remind myself of this fact often.

Chapter 15

Patience

I HAVE TALKED ABOUT FATIGUE AND weight gain, but I have not yet spoken about patience -more specifically, a *lack* of patience! I believe that a lack of patience is another sign of depression. Some might call it irritability, but it is the same thing. You get frustrated easily. I have learned that, in order to be a good parent, you should be patient with your children. This is very difficult when you have two babies within fourteen months of each other. Lack of sleep does not help your patience, especially if one of your children is colicky. That was my situation. Pierre-Hugues was crying most of the time while Cassandra was being the perfect baby, always smiling. I thanked God for her. She made things much easier for us. She did not fuss, she always listened to our instructions, and she even tried to console her little brother. Yes, she was a godsend! Unfortunately, I do not think that I was as patient as I would have liked to be as they grew up.

The older Pierre-Hugues got, the better things got (and the less colicky he was). Between six months and one year, he was a good baby. It was a lot of work to have two young children, but the crisis eased when he began sleeping through the night. My own personal crisis had not passed, though. I was still in the phase of trying out new medication, and I was not getting good results. By the time I went back to work, things had settled down. We had a routine, and life was getting better every day. I did notice, however, that exhaustion reduced my patience. It was very important for me to sleep at least ten hours per night. If I could sleep twelve hours, that was even better. My sleeping schedule meant that Claude had to get up with the children more often than I would. However, we came to an agreement that, on weekends, we would trade off getting up with the kids. Plus, because the children were still taking naps in the afternoon, Claude and I could also nap, which we did religiously.

To this day, my sleep is crucial to my well-being. I require more sleep than the average person does, and I make sure that I get enough. If I do not get enough sleep, I become irritable immediately. I have also seen the depressive symptoms reappear whenever I deprive myself of sleep. This is a weak spot for me, which means I will forever have to make sure that I sleep at least eight hours.

The older the children got, the more patience I required. I must admit that, often, I lacked such patience. I am not proud of that fact, but I have to accept my limits and forgive myself. I do the best that I can, and I cannot expect myself to be more than that. As a perfectionist, this is very difficult for me. I would prefer to be a perfect mother, but that's not possible. When I am tired and running out of patience, I do raise my voice at my children. It does not mean that I do not love my children … it means that I have very distinct limits. I do not spank my children—my husband and I do not believe in spanking. There is no physical or emotional abuse in our house, but you will hear me scream at my children occasionally.

As I said, I am not proud of this, and I am trying to work on this issue. Today, with the help of meditation and reiki healing, I am able to be calmer with my children. (reiki healing is explained in chapter 18)

My daughter (who is now fourteen) knows how to push my buttons. She could easily upset me. By pushing my buttons, though, she helps me deal with issues that are not resolved in my spiritual life. Sometimes I do not even realize that the comment she just made gets to me. I often do not understand why I get upset with her instead of letting it go. Unconsciously, she is helping me heal. The triggers are associated with things that need to change or improve in my life such as letting go and accepting things as they are. I do not need to be right all the time, I can let the comment go and not argue. That is difficult for me because I have been raised believing that you had to defend your point of view if you wanted to be heard. She is helping me grow spiritually. I can only hope that my interactions with her are doing the same. I am hoping that she will be better equipped in life. I am sure that she will have her own struggles; however, I am hoping that my parenting skills are enabling her to better deal with life.

My daughter is mature for her age, and sometimes she speaks to me as if I were the child. Still, she has so much to learn. I try to tell her that my job as a parent is to provide her with tools for life. Your parents, teachers, and friends give you tools that you put in your toolbox, and later on, whenever you need to fix something, you go in your toolbox for the proper tool. The same applies to life: the tools that you are provided with are always there for you. I feel that my job is to provide my children with these tools. Sometimes, your life experience is the tool you give them; sometimes, you find other tools that you have never used before. You could say that my daughter and I are learning some of these tools together—we grow together and learn lessons based on where we are in life.

She is a lot like me, though, so when she says or does something that reminds me of my own shortcomings, it always produces a reaction. Did I have the same effect on my parents? I am more like my father than my mother—did I trigger things in him that caused him to be so impatient with me? I never felt that he loved me. Today, I wonder whether it was because he had a hard time loving himself. I remember being thirteen years old and hating my life. I did not get along with my father, and I felt that he was always against me. The only support I felt came from my mother. My hormones were also unbalanced, and I remember writing in my diary that I hated myself. I also tried to stop breathing. I thought that, if I held my breath, I would die. Of course, I could not stop breathing for more than a few seconds.

I wonder whether my depression started at thirteen (when my hormones were so out there). As I reflect back on those days, I see the whole scenario differently. Both my parents loved me very much, and they tried to raise me the best way possible. If I was unhappy, it was probably because of the hormonal changes in my body. Today, I know that my father loves me. What crazy thoughts I had! If I had looked at my life with a different lens, I would have realized that I had a good life.

I think that my daughter is going through the same challenge (with the changes in her hormones). Since I truly remember how hard it was for me, you would think that I would be able to help her with the changes; yet, I have difficulty understanding her.. How can I help her? I heard somewhere that the best thing you can do for your children at this age is to listen. That is all that they need. It sounds so simple, yet it is so hard to do. We, as parents, want to fix things for our children, so we listen, but we are quick to offer advice—advice that they do not want. I have decided that I will try listening from now on. My son, the difficult child at birth, is very easy to deal with at twelve years old. I wonder if it is because his hormones have not yet kicked in. My daughter (who was perfect for the first ten years of her life) is now more challenging. This is normal, though—it is called puberty.

She is still loving and giving; however, she will throw tantrums occasionally. Therefore, I get it when she tells me that I do not understand her. She is right—I do not understand her. I understand that her behavior is very normal for her age; I just have difficulty accepting the changes in her. It is difficult to see those changes and to understand that she is growing up. I also have a hard time watching my children argue and I find that because she is more sensitive and moody, she can become the instigator. I should not complain about her because she is a good person, and I know that some parents are going through much worse experiences than I am. She is a very good student, and she always gets good grades. All of her teachers adore her! I could see her as a teacher's pet! She takes her responsibilities seriously, and she does not drink or do drugs. She has good friends. Really, I cannot ask for a better daughter. I am just having difficulty coping with the changes in her. She challenges me more now. As I said, she is a normal teenager, and I love her dearly—even when she has her tantrums! I just wish she would be happy all the time as she used to be. I know it is the hormones that are affecting her, but I am beginning to dislike those hormones!

As for my son, he is the opposite. He was difficult at a young age, and now he is purely a godsend. He calms me down.

It is as if he understands my frustrations with his sister—and he tries to make things easier. As I mentioned, they argue a lot these days. I am told this is perfectly normal. Siblings do fight and argue at this age, especially when one has her hormones out of whack. I can just imagine what it will look like once his hormones start to kick in! I am truly lucky to have two wonderful children. We have done a great job raising them—so far, anyway! They are so important to me, and I am sure they do not realize how much.

Patience is a virtue that one must seek at all times. I will forever have to work on this virtue, however. I have often asked myself, *Why is this happening to me?* At the beginning, I had the sense that life was unfair, that life had sent me a challenge that I was not prepared for. Today, I know better. I know that God had a reason; more so, I believe I chose this path before my birth. Some believe that we choose the challenges we want to face in our life. Before birth, we create a roadmap that includes the people we want to live with. I believe in this even though my Catholic upbringing does not accept this type of thinking. I could face my challenge because God made sure that I had the tools to go through it. Most importantly, though, I learned from this difficult time.

What did I learn? I have learned that, when faced with a challenge, everyone can be vulnerable. Depression was a blessing in disguise. This sounds awful, but it is the truth. It made me look at my lack of self-esteem and learn to become less dependent on the people I love. No one could get me out of my depression—I had to do it by myself in the end. Still, I have to admit that I would have never been able to emerge without the proper medication and psychotherapy. The medication helps your brain return to normal. It feeds it serotonin, which a depressed person lacks. The psychotherapy helps you deal with the emotional scars that you have. Many times, these issues are the reason why you became ill. Your body gives you signs, and it's sometimes challenging to listen. I did not listen to my body when it told me it was tired. I did not stop working when I should have. My hormones from the pregnancy did not help the situation. Of course, we do not have any control over our hormones when we are pregnant. To me, the hormones were detrimental—they provoked my migraines and made me an emotional wreck. What I did not realize before was how much of myself I was giving to my job, my family, and my husband. I was not listening to what I truly needed. I did not want to upset my family or my husband, so I would betray myself by refusing to listen to my body or to my wishes. At that time, I had no idea that my soul was screaming at me to listen.

The depression stopped me cold, and it forced me to listen to my body. My body stopped functioning normally, so I had to sleep and be selfish. That was difficult for me because I wanted to be there for my children and take care of them. My recovery probably took longer because of the guilt I was feeling. I only began to forgive myself in 2011 —it took me twelve years to rid myself of the guilt, to accept the illness, and to accept who I have become.

Chapter 16
Long Recovery

I NDEED, IT WAS A LONG recovery because I needed time to heal and live outside the darkness. Once I returned to work full time (four days a week is full time for me), I got back into the busy life we led with the children. We would work our week, and on weekends, we would bring the children to their gymnastics and dance classes (for Cassandra), ball hockey (for Pierre-Hugues), soccer, etc. Our life became busy, which is normal for a family of four. I still did not make time for myself. I had not yet learned my valuable lesson. I still took for granted my health. I was no longer depressed, but I did not take care of myself. Twice, I have noticed the symptoms of depression coming back. This occurred when I tried to work five days a week. Those symptoms stopped me—I did not want to be ill again. Twice, I had to take leave without pay for a month or six weeks and slow down. The minute that I realized where I was going, I made an appointment with my psychiatrist. Every time, he prescribed rest and time away from work for a certain amount of time.

The last time I was on leave, the doctor gave me an assignment. I had to find out what I truly wanted to do with my life. Was my current job fulfilling my needs? I am not speaking about the financial aspect, but rather what my heart truly needed. I did not know it then, but the doctor wanted me to follow my spirit.

Once you follow the guidance from your spirit, you become truly happy. I had to re-evaluate my life, look at what was making me happy, and look at what wasn't working. My need number one is sleep. I cannot function with fewer than eight hours of sleep. My need number two is making time for myself. It does not matter what it is, as long as I take time to do something that I enjoy. It could be reading a romance novel, going for a walk in the woods with my dogs, scrapbooking, or painting. It is difficult to do something only for myself, though—as a mother, I always think of the children.

I do not believe that we can fully recover from depression if we do not take the time to evaluate our life and make changes. As I already said, our bodies speak to us … and if they break down, it is because we need to stop and look at what is not going well. When I started to change my life, my life became better because of the changes. If I refuse to stop to smell the flowers or read a book or take a nap in the afternoon, my body will tell me. This became clearer during my mid-life crisis.

I was finally out of my depression, but I was still tired all the time. This is my family!

Chapter 17
Big Change

THE MOMENT THAT CHANGED MY life occurred in 2010, after we returned from our family trip to Texas. I was upset, doubting myself as a mother and a wife. I was wondering whether I was worthy of love. Deep within my soul, I knew the answer, but my ego would not let me see it. The ego is our self-image, the part that always judges and finds faults in everything. It is essentially the negative voice in your head. The ego might think that it is protecting us; however, it is providing us with self-limiting thoughts. It will force you to jump to conclusions and in the end, will sabotage you. It interferes with you, connecting with your spirit. I had a fight with my husband (he was voicing what my ego was telling me), but I knew that my doubts were not valid. My spirit was telling me a different story. I needed to find myself and see who I was; I needed to uncover my diamond, my spirit. This meltdown indicated that we were not happy; we were frustrated with each other, and we felt plenty of resentment. This was a wake-up call for me. Something needed to change, and I finally realized that I could not change him. In order to uncover my diamond, I had to change. I was extremely emotional, and I needed to know that I would be fine. At first, I was so upset that I did not know where to turn. I panicked, because I felt as if my world had just ended. To hear my husband say he doubted my abilities as a mother aggravated me—maybe even infuriated me. I thought, *If this is what my husband is thinking, I am better off without him.* I did not want him in my life and felt I deserved better. However, I still needed to hear that everything would be fine (even if I separated from my husband). I decided to call Laura, a psychic that I had seen a couple of times, and she was so accurate. (I elaborate on Laura in Chapter 25) I knew she would tell me I would be okay (even if we decided to separate). Deep down in my soul, I knew I would be fine and would come out of my crisis stronger. Still, I just needed someone else to tell me that.

She believed we would stay together, but she told me I had free will and could decide to leave. She indicated that, once I started to change my thinking, my energy would change for the better (along with the relationship). "Work on yourself and things will fall into place," she told me. Working on me meant taking time for myself and learning to love myself. I needed to be gentle with myself. She also indicated that I needed to do some healing energy work—reiki—and do some journey work. She provided me with two names of women who would be able to help me heal. She was a godsend! I truly love this woman. I do not know many people who have such a big heart. Her mission is to help others heal.

Chapter 18
Reiki

THE FIRST TIME I HEARD about reiki was in 2008. A colleague of mine indicated that she was receiving reiki treatments and spoke about how they changed her energy. The minute I heard the word energy my ears opened up! I wanted and needed more energy, as I was tired all the time. I decided that I would try a reiki treatment. Upon my arrival, I noticed that the practitioner's reiki table was essentially the same as a massage table. She told me to lie on my back. The difference between a massage and reiki is that you keep your clothes on for reiki treatment and the practitioner gently lays her/his hands on you, they do not massage you. If you are not comfortable with having their hands on you, they can still do reiki with their hands above you. She explained that reiki is a healing energy that is provided through the hands, more specifically with the fingers. The patient feels heat or warmth coming from the practitioner's hands and goes into the body. Beside from feeling warmth from her hands, I did not feel much more except on occasions, I would feel pain in my lower back. She explained that this was normal; it was simply blocked energy moving from that location. It reminded me of when I had a reflexology treatment. Whenever the practitioner would press a pressure point in my feet, I would feel pain in my body. Pressure points on the feet are directly linked to an area in the body. By pressing the point on your foot, you are releasing pressure from the affected area in your body. For my reiki treatment, she maintained her hands on my stomach, the blockage dissolved, and the pain went away. She was removing the blockage with the energy located in her hands.

One benefit from reiki is that it removes energy blockages from your body. I was a bit disappointed after my first treatment because I did not feel a burst of energy. She did tell me that I needed more than one treatment in order to see an improvement. I saw her three times and then decided I was not going to continue with the treatment. I was not paying attention to what my body needed. I was not yet ready to accept the wonderful gifts of reiki. Two years later, in 2010 after my meeting with Laura, I did open up to the healing process and accept to see Donna.

I met with Donna a week after Laura referred me. She is a reiki master with a degree in social work, and works with women with low self-esteem. We initially spoke about my life and my unhappiness and then proceeded with the reiki treatment. As she was working on me, her guides were telling her that the angels would help me heal. Donna indicated that I should buy myself some angel oracle cards in order to receive messages from the Angels. I obeyed and got myself some Angel Oracle cards by Doreen Virtue. This small step was the start of the big shift in my life. The cards enabled me to receive messages from the angels, and permitted me to follow their guidance. It was easy to use and it brought clarity into my life. I use these cards to this day—I just love Doreen's Virtue's cards and her books. I have healed because of her books and cards.

The reiki treatment cost me eighty-five dollars. I knew that I could not afford to see her every week to have reiki treatments, but I also knew that the treatments were beneficial. Therefore, I decided to take a reiki class with Donna. Before I started the classes, I needed to feel completely at ease with this direction. I had an inner struggle; I was torn between following my inner guidance or following what the Catholic Church dictates. The Catholic Church does not embrace certain alternative methods of healing such as reiki. I had many discussions with family and friends, some were supportive, and others were completely opposed with me practicing reiki. This internal debate brought me to seek counsel from my childhood priest. I asked his views on the matter. He acknowledged that some people do not approve of reiki mainly because some practitioners abuse its powers. However, he shared with me that he had a close friend that did reiki and he did not have an issue if I were to practice it. I remember asking him if I would go to hell if I practiced reiki. He assured me that I would not because of my intentions which are pure. After this discussion, I felt much better about pursuing my reiki classes.

My good friend Gabriel decided to take the class with me, so both of us started our reiki journey together. We took a beginning reiki class with Donna, and we received an attunement. I had to practice every day. It was part of the class assignment, and it turned out to be very beneficial for me. Reiki gave me inner strength, but most of all, it gave me peace. I started to meditate with reiki. I was able to relax and let go of the stress in my life. It transformed my life! Because I had to practice every day, I needed to take some time just for me every day. This was difficult for the children to understand because they were used to having access to their mommy whenever they wanted. I explained to them that, whenever my bedroom door was closed that meant that I was doing my reiki and could not be disturbed. I took one hour per day to practice. This hour per day was dedicated to me in order to relax and meditate while doing my reiki. It gave me the opportunity to know my body, and it provided me with insight about my physical tension. I also learned how to release it. It was truly a healing exercise.

Reiki is a way to relax and release tension or help with pain. It also enabled me to remain healthy. While doing reiki, I am more connected with my body and this connection keeps me away from depression. I immediately feel any sign of stress or pressure and I listen to what my body is trying to tell me. I would love to say that I use it every day; unfortunately, I am not disciplined enough to do so. Still it has taught me to pay attention to my body (beyond pain). Reiki is good for both the mind and the body. It showed me how to meditate and to concentrate on one point in my body at a time. The first time I felt the energy go through my fingers, I was amazed and loved the feeling. As my daughter would say, it was cool! Reiki centers the mind while releasing whatever needs releasing—blockages, toxins, negative energy. You do not need to worry about what to do; the universe is doing all the work. The person practicing reiki is the enabler; he or she is the conduit between the universe and the client. The energy comes from the universe through the hands and into the client's body.

I decided to pursue my knowledge and took a second-level reiki class. With that class, I learned how to practice reiki on other people. What I love about reiki is that I can heal someone without having to know what to do. I just listen to my intuition and rest my hands where I am compelled to rest them … the universe does the rest. I have learned that the reiki practitioner receives a treatment while giving a treatment. That is bonus points! I have practiced on my children and on Pongo.Claude did not let me do reiki on him in the beginning. I believe that the whole concept was too foreign for him. I also attended a reiki share every month. There, groups of reiki practitioners meet and do mini-reiki treatments on each other. This has provided me with confidence in my abilities. Shortly after I completed my second-level reiki class, I enrolled in the third level. I wanted to pursue this learning. It brought me so many benefits, and I felt I needed to proceed with my journey. Every time you advance a level, your healing energy increases. For me, I felt more energy with every attunement. I started to practice reiki with my friends, and they were surprised at the beautiful healing. It also increased my spiritual beliefs. It is funny but it actually expanded my spirituality. It brought me closer to my spirit and to God. In connecting with my spirit and God, it helped me heal emotionally. Whenever I seek counsel or feel hurt emotionally, I practice reiki. It grounds me and brings me back to the basics. It provides me with guidance on how to proceed. Reiki has brought that connection. I call it my spiritual guidance. It also made me more conscious of others and their well-being. I am more compassionate because of this new consciousness.

Today, I am a reiki master. This means that, I can provide reiki treatments to people *and* teach others. I wanted to become a reiki master because I wanted to be able to share the special gift with Pierre-Hugues. He has shown interest in reiki from the beginning, and I decided that he was ready to learn the basics. I have attuned Pierre-Hugues to the first level. I have taught him the basic information about the healing benefits and the different chakras in the body. He has learned how to activate the healing energy and where to put his hands for the treatment. He understands that reiki is special, and he does not abuse it. He can do reiki on himself, and he can do it on others. I sometime ask him to do reiki on me when I feel pain. It is funny to feel the heat coming from his tiny hands. It goes to show you that anyone interested in learning reiki can learn it and apply it. I trust that, eventually, he will want to learn more—at that time, he can advance to the next level. For now, he is content where he is.

If thirteen years ago, I had been opened to alternative medicine such as reiki, it would have helped me tremendously during my depression. Unfortunately, I did not know that reiki existed. I am convinced that reiki treatments can benefit someone that is suffering from depression. Whenever I feel stressed or tired, reiki helps me to relax and brings me calmness. I feel rejuvenated after a treatment. The beauty of it is that the treatments are free as I am able to provide myself with treatments anywhere, anytime. I have given myself a reiki treatment in an airplane! I could feel a migraine coming and I did not want to be sick. I had to take action right away so I started to do reiki on myself. It worked as the pain was reduced considerably. Speaking of migraines, I still suffer from them. I have tried many medications but nothing truly worked until I found reiki and acupuncture. Acupuncture is another alternative healing treatment that is not well known. After approximately eight months of treatments, I am virtually migraine free! The healing power of acupuncture is immense. It can heal many things (including muscle pain). It can also boost your immune system and help with anxiety, depression, and many other things. I am certain that someone suffering from depression would find relief from this alternative medicine. Someone had recommended that I see an acupuncturist when I was pregnant with Cassandra in order to relieve me of my migraines. I refused! I was not ready to follow the alternative healing medicine route. However, today with my experience with both reiki and acupuncture, I truly believe that if you join both of them, you have a winning combination as a treatment.

I have created a beautiful room in my house in which I can do reiki treatments. I just love that room! It is so peaceful in there! My goal is to start a mini-practice at home. I would love to teach others and provide treatments. I also want to bring awareness to the benefits of reiki. Someday, I will be able to quit my job and do healing work full time. I believe that this will be more fulfilling than my present job. However, I do not have enough clients at this time to do reiki full time.

Chapter 19

Journey Work

I WAS FORTUNATE TO MEET WITH Marie-Sylvie, the person Laura recommended for a journey process. I did not know at the time that Marie-Sylvie is also a psychologist. She proved to be invaluable to me. Before I met her, she wanted me to read a book by Brandon Bays, *The Journey.* The book is the biography of Brandon Bays, where she explains how she was able to cure her cancer with the journey process. It is remarkable! She had stomach cancer—the tumor was the size of a basketball—and she was able to cure it within six weeks. That is the power of the journey. The process requires confronting a painful memory that is "stuck" in your body. Through the journey process, you are able to reprogram this memory into a positive one. In order to heal, you need to forgive. When you forgive, your memory cell is reprogrammed. This means that, somewhere in your body, you have healed a cell. Your pain disappears, and you are healed. Some people have recovered from blindness, but I recovered from my irritable bowel syndrome. I was no longer constipated, and that was huge for me.

Marie-Sylvie was able to shed some light on my life, on what I truly wanted in my life. We discussed my marriage, my children, my depression, and my childhood. After many sessions, I made up my mind that I no longer wanted the married life that I had. I wanted to leave Claude. I was ready, and I knew that I would be fine living without him. I wanted to be independent and make my own decisions without having to compromise. Marie-Sylvie cautioned me to take my time before making a drastic decision.

Claude and I had a discussion one Friday night about our married life and what we wanted. We both agreed that it would be best for everyone if we separated. It was getting emotional, so I left the room, went upstairs, and did reiki on myself. The process was so strong—I had never felt that way before. I kept saying to myself, *I am loved, and everything is fine.* With every inhalation, I would repeat that affirmation, and with every exhalation, I would say *All the sadness and fear comes out of me.* I probably did reiki for thirty or fifty minutes, and afterwards, I felt whole and relaxed.

I returned downstairs to Claude. I was peaceful, not at all emotional. We started to discuss the details of our separation. We needed to decide on living arrangements, visitation for the children, and which items we wanted to keep. Because it was one week before Christmas, we decided that we would not tell the children before the New Year began. That night, however, I told my parents about the separation. The next day, I needed to buy myself a car because we only had one vehicle. I needed to buy something that was not too expensive, so I bought myself a Jetta. That night, upon my return, I found Claude in the basement, cleaning out some boxes. He seemed sad. I told him about my purchase and asked him how he was. He indicated that he was sad and did not sleep that well the previous night. Until the previous night, I do not think that he had truly thought about the implication of a separation.

That night, when he came to bed, I had an urge to snuggle up to him, so I did so. I did not know what to expect from him. He responded to me with urgency, and we connected like never before. That night changed everything for us. It was as if we found each other again. We needed each other, and we realized that we still loved each other. Needless to say, we never separated. From that day forward, we took it one day at a time and spent Christmas together.

Shortly after, I received an e-mail regarding travel deals, and I proposed to Claude that we leave for a week and reconnect. He was not really in favor of leaving the children, as usual. I spoke about it with my parents, and they were convinced that it was a great idea. They immediately told us they would babysit the kids, and my father convinced Claude to go. We got ourselves a great deal! We only spent thirteen hundred dollars to stay a week in Mexico in a five star hotel! We left the following weekend, spent a week together without the children, and relaxed. It was nice to get away and just spend time with each other. However, we did have a fight. Marie-Sylvie said we probably would. "Just take it as it is," she said. It was just a fight, nothing major. I dealt with the issue and moved on. That was a new approach for me—I usually dwelled on things. In sum, it was a week to heal and put the past behind us.

Chapter 20
Letting Go

My beloved Pongo! My best friend, I miss you so much!

JANUARY 3 2011, WAS A difficult day: we had to send Pongo to heaven. He was in a great deal of pain (emanating from his hips), and the previous night, he started to cry out while motionless. It was so sad. We did not want to see him die, but we promised ourselves that we would not let him suffer. We tried different medications, and during his last week, we gave him painkillers. It was obvious that they were not working, and we had to make a big decision. On that Monday night, we had to let him go. It was an extremely emotional night; we wanted to be with him until the end, so we stayed with Pongo at the veterinary hospital until his last breath. I kept kissing him and telling him how much I loved him. I thanked him for always being there for me. He was my true best friend; he was there for me all these years and especially during my depression. He provided me with unlimited love and affection (without ever judging me or asking for anything in return). He was my first-born baby, and I treated him as my child. As I write this, I still have tears in my eyes. I miss him dearly, and I still speak to him. He was my rock for so many years—how do you leave a loved one?

I held him in my arms and cried. As I told him I loved him, he passed away. Claude was devastated; he was not ready to let go of him. To this day, he says that we should not have let him die right away. Pongo could have lived longer, but at what price? He would have suffered longer. We did the right thing. Anyway, a trip to Mexico helped us forget the difficult situation, so the timing was perfect in that sense.

Chapter 21
The Journey

A T THE END OF JANUARY 2011, I participated in a journey weekend. The weekend was an in-depth experience in practicing journey processes. As I previously explained, the journey process heals at the cellular level. I had done journeywork individually with Marie-Sylvie, but that was the first time I explored journey processes with a group. They started the weekend by explaining the two different types of journey processes: the first was physical and the second was emotional. Both processes produce the same results. They helped reprogram the cellular memory. The difference between the two processes is the means to get there. I did two or three journey processes during that weekend, and I got great results. I was finally able to forgive myself. I needed to forgive myself for being depressed. As if I had any decision in the matter! It is funny how our minds work sometimes.

I learned that I did not think I was a good mother. I was able to understand that I did not need to be a perfect mother; I just needed to be me—that was enough for my children. I forgave myself for having weaknesses, and I was finally able to accept my depression. I was able to accept that, as a human being, I had limits, and it was perfectly fine to have such limits.

Before the weekend, I did not feel worthy of Cassandra's love, as if something inside myself was preventing me to accept her love. During the weekend I realized that what was preventing me from accepting someone else's love was because I did not love myself. The reason why I did not love myself was that I thought I was a bad mother and a weak person. That could not be furthest from the truth. Once I made that realization, I was able to forgive myself. After I forgave myself, I was able to love myself and truly see myself for who I really am, a beautiful strong woman. It actually takes strength to live through depression. I was not weak, that is not the reason why depression striked. It was because I was lost; I was denying my spirit to come out into the world. That is one of the reasons for my depression, not weakness. As a result, I became a stronger person to have lived through this painful experience. Once all of this was revealed, I was able to love myself as much as she loved me. That weekend changed my life. It was very emotional. I cried a lot—forgiveness is a healing process so strong that I cannot describe it. I can only say that I received inner peace after I forgave myself. That is what truly healed me and changed my life. Without the journey, I would not have been able to forgive myself (or it would have taken me much longer).

The weekend was the start of my new journey. It was the start of loving myself as I am. I learned to stop judging and accept myself completely. I continued to visit my psychotherapist and work on healing my wounds. We started to peel the onion, so to speak. I learned that, whenever I was hurt, I built a wall around my heart. It was time to bring those walls down by gently healing the wound and peeling the onion. The more layers I dropped, the closer I got to my true spirit. I learned that accepting myself is the key to happiness. In addition, the tools I gained access to during the weekend are always available to me. There are monthly meetings where you can share the journey process with others. If you are interested in journey work, you can find information at the following website: http:// thejourneyna.com/.

Chapter 22

My True Self, My Diamond

I READ A BOOK WRITTEN BY Sonia Choquette that inspired me to find my true self. There are many words for your true self: your spirit, your higher self, etc. In the journey process, we call it our diamond. I have used all of these words throughout my book. Regardless, it is important to find your true self. Most of us spend our life trying to discover whom we truly are within. During the last few years I have started to discover who I truly am. With the help of meditation, reiki, the journey process and psychotherapy, I have made some wonderful discoveries about myself.

It can be difficult to accept that you are beautiful inside, that you have a precious diamond in your heart. It is especially difficult if you have been criticizing yourself all your life. I have the bad habit of looking at my weaknesses and not acknowledging the beautiful qualities I possess. I guess perfectionists often feel that way. I have sabotaged myself all my life with my negative thoughts, thanks to my ego! With the help of Louise Hay's book on positive affirmation, I started to speak to myself in a more positive way. I started to leave myself sticky notes around the house with positive affirmations on them. I have also shared some of her oracle cards with my daughter (she also has the tendency to see the negative rather than the positive).

I started to read many self-help books. My favorite authors are Louise Hay, Sonia Choquette, and Doreen Virtue. I also enjoy their meditation CDs. I have started to discover my spirit thanks to Sonia. I have started to pray to the angels thanks to Doreen and I have changed my inner thoughts thanks to Louise. My journey consisted of applying some principles that I learned (in the books I read) and applying what Marie-Sylvie taught me. I had to search within myself and recognize my strengths. I had to accept that I was not perfect, and I had to choose how to improve myself. Perception is the key. How you perceive things will help you change your behavior. If you only see the negative things in life, you will remain a negative person. I started a gratefulness diary. Each day, I wrote at least ten things for which I was grateful. This forced me to look at the positive in my life. It changed my perception. It was as if I had changed optic lenses. The world was a better place to live. It was more beautiful than the day before. Praying also helped me with my journey. I reconnected with God and told Him how thankful I was to have a beautiful life.

After surviving depression, you can see the beauty in many things. I appreciate life instead of merely living it. God is with me every day, and I make an effort to speak to Him and thank Him every day. It is as if my journey brought me closer to Him. During depression, I do not recall being close to Him, but today, He is with me daily. I understand that I am on this earth for a reason, and only He knows what that is. Sometimes, He gives me clues, but I have faith that He will bring me closer to my diamond.

Chapter 23

Meditation

R EIKI HAS OPENED MY MIND to meditation. I try to meditate a few hours per week, and I journal the thoughts that result from meditation. While doing this, I noticed that I was receiving messages from my guides and angels. Doreen's book explains how to listen to your angels' messages. One summer, while meditating, I received a message telling me to write a book about my life (concentrating on my depression). I was taken aback because I never considered myself to be a good writer, and I never considered writing a book about myself. I never really enjoyed writing, and I wondered why people would want to know my life story. I am an ordinary woman who struggled with depression. So what? No big thing—others have suffered a lot more than I have. However, surprisingly, I did not question the message. I have always believed that my depression happened for a reason … maybe the reason was to help others by sharing my experience. The other message that came through that day was that I needed to go to a tropical island to meditate and do research for my book. That trip would help me heal.

Every day, I listen to one of Doreen's meditation CDs: *Chakra Clearing.* That meditation allows you to clear all seven chakras. She has a morning and evening meditation. While driving to work, I use the morning meditation and visualize myself clearing out all my negative energy. I feel more prepared for the day. I meditate also when I need answers. I will ask a question to the universe, and then I will meditate on it. I always receive an answer. Sometimes, however, I am not ready to receive the answer (or I doubt it). For example, I was not prepared to write about myself. Doing so brought me outside my comfort zone. I did not start to write immediately, but the message to write kept coming back to me.

During one of her sessions, Laura told me I needed to write a book about my life. Did I start laughing at that one! I told her that I had received that message myself while meditating. The universe made sure that I heard the message and followed through. I did not know where to start. I meditated and asked Archangel Gabriel to guide me with the writing. He came through. Many times, I just started writing, not knowing what word would come next—my fingers just moved as the words formed in my mind. I know that this book was written with the help of God and His angels. I understand that this concept may be foreign to many of you. It is also foreign to my husband—he believes in God, but when I start to talk about my angels, he likes to make fun of me. I see that he is not totally on the same page. That is okay because it is my journey, not his. My meditation brings me peace and makes me happy. That is what truly counts; it makes me a better person.

Chapter 24

Hawaii

T HAT TROPICAL ISLAND ENDED UP being the Big Island of Hawaii. I knew that my trek would not be a tropical getaway, though. The trip would be a personal journey to find myself and heal. I wanted to go by myself, but my mother would not let me! Yep, I was over forty years old, and my mother still worried about me! She decided to come with me because we had never travelled together (without others). I searched the Internet to find a place to stay—I knew that I did not want to stay in a hotel. I came across a little house located in the rainforest. It faced the ocean. The minute I saw the house, I knew it was the house for my journey. It was perfect! It had no electricity, no telephone, and no television.

The house was located in an area that did not have electricity. It had solar panels and propane gas for the stove. I continued to search for a house; however, I knew that I had found the right one. I contacted the owner and asked whether the house was available in September. Before he even answered the question, I knew that it was vacant. My gut had already told me that it would be the one. I loved the idea of going back to nature, being surrounded by a rainforest and the ocean. I packed my bags with many self-help books, including ones by Sonia Choquette. I brought my yoga pad and some clothing, and off I went!

The trip took twenty-four hours. Hawaii is far away—the time difference for me was six hours. I am not ashamed to say that I was exhausted by the time we arrived in Hawaii. We spent one night in Honolulu, Oahu because every commercial flight lands in Honolulu. There, I saw an amazing sunrise. I was sitting by the ocean in Honolulu at five o'clock in the morning. The sky was orange, and the sun came up behind Diamond Head (the volcano located by the beach in Honolulu). It was magical! I walked on the white sand beach, and of course, I had to touch the water—previously, we always swam in the Atlantic Ocean. We had a chance to walk around the hotel and see stores before they opened. Our flight was at nine o'clock in the morning for Hilo, (on the Big Island). We did not have much time to visit Honolulu. We took a small plane to get to Hilo—the same type of plane that we usually take from Ottawa to Toronto. The only thing we saw from the airplane window was sea and a bit of land. We flew over Maui, and it looked like a deserted island from up there. We finally arrived in Hilo and drove to our little house in the rainforest. It was fabulous! It was small but perfect. I loved that house! I wished that I could move to a tropical island and have a house exactly like that one. I didn't mind the lack of electricity, phones, and television. It would be marvelous to live a simple life in the tropics. That is my cherished dream. Maybe once the children are old enough to leave home, I will be able to live on a tropical island.

It was truly a beautiful place. We did not need the electricity. I woke early and went to bed early. I usually started my day by meditating, doing yoga, and going for a walk in the beautiful rainforest. During my walks, I received guidance from my higher self (or from God). One morning, while walking in the rainforest, I started to notice leaves in the shape of a heart. They were everywhere—in the middle of the street, in the trees! Finally, I said aloud, "Okay! I get it! You want me to love myself and accept myself the way I am." What a beautiful way to show me that I was loved and should love myself. That morning, God gave me a message to start loving myself. I have to admit that it was not easy, and I struggled with that aim throughout my trip. I also cried a lot. As I said, the trip to Hawaii was not meant to be a tropical retreat. It was a journey to heal myself. *How could I love and heal others if I did not love myself?* I wondered. That message came through very strongly. My mission for the trip was revealed: I had to work on my self-worth and begin to fully love myself.

The fabulous hot pond.

I occupied my time with some leisure activities, such as swimming in hot ponds. That park was magical! It looked like a handmade Olympic pool with hot water. It was a natural gift to the people of the island. The island has two active volcanoes, and they have erupted many times. The lava rocks are everywhere—they cover the forests and the shores. Because the lava rocks can warm the ocean's water, they can create hot ponds. For security purposes, the locals built a wall with a small opening that lets the ocean come through. The water is about ninety degrees Fahrenheit. The pond near the cottage was perfect because we could not swim in the ocean (there were no sandy beaches on our side of the island, and the waves would have been too strong). I went to the hot pond and swam my heart out! Sometimes, I just sunbathed or read my book. Another form of relaxation entailed sitting on the lava rocks by the ocean. The ocean almost touched my feet, and I found it pleasurable to read or meditate while listening to the waves.

I knew that it was going to be a journey, but I was still surprised at how emotional I became. I must have been shedding some onion layers! The tears were probably washing away any wounds. I have to confess that I was not good company for my mother. I was moody and irritable. My psychologist told me that it was perfectly normal for me to act that way, that it was part of the healing process. It was as if I had to get the negative toxins out of my body. And they manifested via an irritable mood.

I experienced my first water massage while in Hawaii. That was out of this world! I do not think that we have that type of massage in Canada. I released a lot during that massage. Many emotions went through (and eventually left) my body. The massage was therapeutic and exactly what I needed. I needed to release blockages and negative feelings. It was all part of the plan. I do not think I knew what the plan was, but I was following my gut. It helped that I was reading Trust Your Vibes by Sonia Choquette. I followed any signs or guidance I received. One afternoon, I had a strong feeling that I should call home. Because we did not have a phone at the house, we had to call from a payphone in the city. That day, the feeling was so strong that I got in the car and immediately drove to the nearest payphone. Because of the six hours difference, it was late in Ottawa—around eleven o'clock at night. My husband answered. He seemed stressed, and he was relieved to speak with me. An incident had occurred at the school, and my husband was not pleased about it. He was happy to be able to share the story with me. I needed to call because my husband needed me at that precise time. I was glad that I followed my gut instinct.

Chapter 25
Psychic Abilities

I HAVE ALWAYS BEEN ATTRACTED TOWARDS psychics and the concept of seeing the future. I remember that around the age of eight years old, I learned a trick with a needle and a thread. It was telling us how many children we would have, depending on how the needle would move above our hand. I was captivated by this trick! According to the needle, I was to have four children. Well, it was not quite accurate. Today, every time I see pendulums I remember those days with the thread and the needle. Later on, as a teenager, my cousin and I would do readings with plain old playing cards. She had a book that described what the cards meant. We spent hours reading for each other and during a period, it was every day. As an adult, I have seen approximately four different psychics. Some were reading in a teacup, others would have you write on a piece of paper your questions and you would burn it in a fireplace and others would just connect and read. My favorite and the most accurate psychic is of course Laura. A colleague of mine recommended her. The reading she gave him was so accurate that I immediately wanted to meet her. The first time I saw her I did not know what to expect. She explained that she connects with her guides and they provide her with information. She told me things that no one would have the ability to know. That is when I knew she was authentic. She provided me with some predictions and some guidance. Her predictions came true, I managed to secure the position that I wanted. She described me the person I should seek in order to obtain that position. Based on her description it was very easy to find who she was talking about. What I love about her is that she provides you with background information about yourself, which confirms that she is real, but then she not just provides you with information about the future, but rather information on how you can have a better life. She is more a spiritual guide. I have grown so much because of her guidance. She provided me with tools on how to improve my life. For example, I have changed my eating habits; I eat much healthier thanks to her guidance. She has reassured me many times; one of these times was when my husband and I were going through a difficult time. She also provided me with reassurance regarding my children. I sometimes doubted my decisions about them and when I spoke to her about my concerns, she was able to reassure me that I was on the right path.

The first time I did a reading was during a reiki class with crystals. The teacher provided us with a crystal ball and asked us to follow our inner thoughts and share them with others. My partner asked me a question, and I briefly meditated while holding the crystal. I did not see images in my mind; however, I heard thoughts—as if someone were talking to me. I started to repeat the words I heard inside my head. After my reading, my partner shared with me that everything I told her made sense. I was amazed! I could become a psychic if I wanted. This was major for me! I was so captivated by being able to connect that I attentively read Sonia's book, *The Life of a Psychic,* and I started to do some exercises. I found out that Sonia Choquette was coming to Montreal. I was excited! I would have an opportunity to be in the same room as her! The day was magical! Sonia is an amazing woman! Her energy is pure, full of love. I do not have the words to explain how loving she is. She truly wants to help everyone have a better life. If we had more people like Sonia, the world would be a better place. Sonia gave us some exercises to do. She made us dance and sing, but most of all, we had *fun*. What a great way to learn! The cherry on top of the sundae was that Sonia met everyone who wanted an autograph at the end of the day. I was one of them. I told her how much I admired her and hoped I could be more like her. Her words of advice to me were as follows: "Practice, practice, and practice." If I wanted to become a psychic, I needed to practice following my gut instincts.

My amazing day with Sonia Choquette.

It is funny how the universe works. During that time, I received an email from Laura. She was hosting a workshop on psychic abilities. I immediately registered and attended. I was starting my psychic journey. During the workshop, we learned to meditate, balance our chakras, and trust our instincts when we received information. People tend to doubt themselves. We do not believe that what we observe is true information; we think our minds are playing tricks on us. Laura explained to us that, by meditating and clearing our chakras, we could open the channel to receive information from our higher self, God, and the angels. We just had to trust ourselves and pay attention to the messages that came through. Sometimes, we do not like what we see or hear, but if the message comes to you more than once, you must accept that the message is truly coming from God.

Today whenever I am uncertain, about anything, I meditate or I connect in order to receive my answers. I do not need to see Laura to reassure me, she has taught me how I can do it by myself. This new tool of channeling is valuable for me. It enables me to connect with my spirit or higher self and truly listen to what is best for me. We often do things to accommodate others but we forget ourselves. If I do what is truly best for me, then others will benefit because I am taking care of myself. This is a very new concept for me. My belief was that as a mother, you are taught that your children come first and you must do everything for them. I am not saying that is untrue. What I am saying is that by making sure your own needs are taken care of, you will be better equipped to take care of others. If I am sick or depressed, how can I take care of my family? If I deny my basic needs, I will become resentful and eventually become sick because I have ignored them. When I speak of my basic needs, I speak of taking time for myself such as going out with a friend or reading a book or sleeping. If I am fulfilling my basic needs and doing something fun, I will be a healthier and a happier person. The time that I meditate or channel is a personal desire and it is fulfillment for my soul. If I deprive myself of that special time because my daughter or son wants me to play a game at that exact moment, I will be frustrated because I was not able to take time for myself and I will not truly enjoy the time spent with them. Instead, I have decided to meditate and spend quality time with them later on. I believe that quality is much better than quantity.

Sonia Choquette and Doreen Virtue often say that messages coming from God or your angels are positives. If you are receiving negative messages, you know that those messages are coming from your ego self. Angels always send messages full of love. They are here to assist us, to help us becoming our true self. They want us to follow our life's mission. I believe that Oprah has mentioned that we are here on earth for a reason, and we must follow our path. I was ready to find out about my life's purpose. Through meditation and channeling, I discovered that my life's purpose was to teach and write. Part of my life's purpose was to write a book about my life and explain the impacts of depression. As you can see, I have started to follow my life's purpose by writing this book. My full-time job does not consist of writing books—and I do not know if I will ever write another one, however I would like to teach or become a public speaker. With this book I hope to fulfill this dream.

Now that I have started my journey to find my true self, I must admit that I am impatient to follow my life's purpose full time. I must be patient and follow my path through the guidance I receive daily from God, my angels, and my spirit guides. Certain meditations have led me to meet them. It is wonderful to feel that you are never alone, that you have a whole team pulling for you. Never before did I realize this. I consistently ask them to help me with my life. Some days, I ask them to help me find a perfect parking spot by the office, and on other days, I ask them to assist my loved ones. Lately, my son has developed some anxiety. I prayed and asked them to help him during those difficult times. I noticed that, whenever I called upon them, his days seemed to be better. I wish that I had known that when I was depressed. It would have lifted some weight off my shoulders. To know that you are never alone and that you are loved no matter what is truly wonderful. It reminds me of a story I learned when I was a child. The story depicts God walking on the beach with a man. The man sees his footsteps in the sand along with another set of footsteps, and he knows that it is God beside him. Then he sees that there is only one set of footsteps in the sand. He says to God, "Why have you left me in this time of need?" God replies, "I have not left you, my child. I am carrying you in this time of need." I can tell you that God has carried me many times, and I am grateful to have him in my life.

Today, I try to teach my children to pray to God and ask the angels for anything that they need in order to make their life easier. I have also taught them a simple exercise to connect and seek guidance. Laura taught this exercise during a workshop. My daughter thinks the exercise is cool. I would like them to start listening to their gut feelings and follow through with their inner guidance. This was not common practice when I grew up. Today I still find it difficult to listen to my inner guidance. I was not taught to think this way. If my children can develop this ability at a young age, it will be for their benefit.

If you truly follow your inner guidance, you always make the right choices.

Something else I have learned during my journey is the benefits of crystals. During my reiki course with crystals, I have learned of their healing powers by simply placing them near us. I have started to use crystals around the house. Both my son and daughter sleep with crystals beside their beds. They bring comfort and healing benefits during the night. I also use crystals during my reiki sessions when I feel that the patient will benefit from them. I have discovered a new world in the last few years with reiki, meditation, channeling and crystals. My life fourteen years ago was so different of how it is today, it is incredible! I am more centered, connected, and most of all, I am much happier with my life. I see these discoveries as tools to enhance my life. Whenever I feel stressed or depressed, I can go into my new toolbox and fix what is wrong or I can seek help if needed. I know that I can ask for help and that is perfectly healthy to do so.

I truly value my new friendships made during this new journey. They provide me with support and love. I consider myself lucky to have met so many wonderful and kind people. These new friends love me for who I truly am without judging me. They also support me when I need them. I thank God for bringing them to me. I wish everyone would have a support group as I do.

Chapter 26

Healing Powers

I HAVE TO SHARE A FUNNY story about my skeptic husband. He did not believe in reiki, crystals, or psychic abilities. I was fortunate that he supported me in my journey even though he did not believe in it. Last summer—the day before we left for Myrtle Beach—he was washing the car. He twisted his ankle and could barely walk on it. He continued to wash the car in great pain. Once he finished, I told him to lie down and let me work on him. He must have been in great pain because he let me do reiki on him! I did a reiki treatment with some crystals for approximately twenty minutes. I kissed him goodnight and went to bed. The next day, we left for Myrtle Beach, and I completely forgot that he had hurt himself. In the car, while driving, my husband turned to me and said, "Brigitte, you are a healer!" I said, "What?" It's funny that I did not understand what he meant by his comment. He explained to me that, miraculously, his ankle no longer hurt. The pain had disappeared! He could not believe it. Now he believes in the healing powers of reiki.

I have come a long way. During my depression years, I would have never thought myself to be capable of healing people. Fourteen years later, I am starting that journey. I have spent the last fourteen years learning about myself—especially how to love myself. It takes time to feel whole. We take many detours throughout our lives, but that is how we learn to live and experience life. Today, I do not regret my depression. I embrace the journey that has led me to today. I can see a diamond in my heart, and I know that I am truly a beautiful person. I am God's child, one of His creations. I will continue to follow my life's purpose ... wherever it leads me. I have faith that God will guide me every step of the way. I also know that the angels will be there to protect me and guide me in my life's purpose. A new life awaits, and I am truly looking forward to it.

I have finally found the real me! I am beautiful, healthy, and happy in my body. Most importantly, I now love myself.

My beautiful family with my golden retrievers!

**God bless you! May you find your
true self and life's purpose.**

CPSIA information can be obtained at www.ICGtesting.com
Printed in the USA
LVOW06s2309081113

360636LV00001B/208/P